How China Thinks

Then and Now

Jacob G Ghazarian

Clink
Street

London | New York

Other titles by Dr. Ghazarian

The Armenian Kingdom in Cilicia During the Crusades:
The integration of Cilician Armenians with the Latins 1080-1393
ISBN 0-7007-1418-9
2000

The Mediterranean Legacy in Early Celtic Christianity:
A journey from Armenia to Ireland
ISBN 1-898948-70-4
2006

Turkey: The heritage of the land
ISBN 978-07552-1172-2
2009

Treasures of the Silk Road
The Religions that Transformed China
ISBN 978-1-910053-43-0
2014

Contents

A Note to the Reader

Throughout this book the reader will find comparative numerical data used to indicate percentages, distances or currency. The sources of such information are referenced accordingly in the Bibliography whenever they were considered proper and scholarly. However, in the course of research conducted for the compilation of this book, often numerical information collected for use was extracted from published materials in daily broadsheets or from their brief editorials which may have been merely drafts, or at best estimates, published for convenience. Hence, such sources were not considered appropriate references and therefore are not cited. The reader is encouraged to view such information with thoughtful reserve, though this does not diminish the value of the context in which the information is used.

With regard to Chinese personal names, it is to be noted that in the literature by-and-large names are conventionally written with the person's surname first followed by the given name as in Mao Tsetung (Mao Zedong) and Deng Xiaoping. However, considering the format of names written in Chinese characters, I have opted to maintain a closer connection with that format and separate the characters of the first names and write the names mentioned above as Mao Tse Tung (or Dong) and Deng Xiao Ping, and likewise all other Chinese personal names that appear.

Acknowledgements

It is imperative that I begin my acknowledgements by first citing the work of the British journalist and academic - Martin Jacques, titled When China Rules the World, first published in 2010 by Penguin Books Limited, London. This remarkable and no less essential guide to understanding the rise of China was the single most significant impetus for my interest in the making of China. My previous publication, titled Treasures of the Silk Road: The Religions that Transformed China, published in 2014, as well as the subject of this book, are a direct result of my fascination with Martin Jacques' insightful descriptions of the fundamentals of the Chinese culture and of its non-Western uniquely different social aspects. Here I include a small part of Martin Jacques' seminal talk entitled Understanding the Rise of China delivered in the TED Salon in London in October 2010: 'Now I know it is a widespread assumption in the West that, as countries modernise, they also Westernise. This is an illusion. It's an assumption that modernity is a product simply of competition, markets and technology. It is not; it is also shaped equally by history and culture. China is not like the West, and it will not become like the West. It will remain in very fundamental respects very different. Now the big questions here are obviously: How do we make sense of China? How do we try to understand what China is? And the problem we have in the West at the moment by-and-large is that the conventional approach is that we understand it really in Western terms, using Western ideas. We cannot'. It is hoped that this small quotation will offer substantial background material in order to aid the reader in focusing on the objectives of this book. Collectively, I see these publications not as personal besotted writings but rather as series of important public service agendas.

Needless to say, I also consider the work of Mark Leonard, titled What Does China Think? a major contribution which I have cited in Chapter II. It, likewise, educates the Western reader on the nuances of the Chinese social norms and on the internal workings of the Chinese communist political system.

Finally, my many thanks go to my colleagues at Wolfson College, particularly to Ellen Rice and Elizabeth Baird whose careful review and corrections of the text are greatly valued. To my friend Jack Walles I owe much for his repeated encouragements and interest in the progress of my writing especially when quality time for writing was hard to come by. In the end, I am eternally grateful to them all.

Introduction

The current *status quo* of the American public is seen as a consequence of decades of wars in Vietnam, Iraq, Afghanistan, Libya and Syria; it has been likened to a person suffering from a hangover after a binge-drinking event the night before. This has given the impetus to the call from the general public for some form of limited isolationism and withdrawal from world policing. But what would be the implications of a limited American isolationism? Consider the political mayhem in Syria, and the sociopolitical unrest it has created in many European nations as being indicative of the potential perils of US inaction. Should we ask whether there are considerably more geopolitical difficulties looming over the horizon for the US? Clearly, there is widespread concern about the phenomenal rise in the People's Republic of China's international stature and the economic wealth it has accumulated in three short decades. But is American isolationism relevant to China's political aspirations? Does the People's Republic of China aspire to rule the world, and if so, when, how and why? Will China one day directly challenge the United States' hegemony? Since the 1980s the United States had enthusiastically helped and supported China in all manners of its economic reforms, industrialisation and modernisation in the belief that a rising China will inevitably lead to a more affluent society that would reject communism and come closer to a cooperative coexistence with the West and expectedly engage in amicable diplomacy with the US. This assumed inevitability was projected to occur under the economic auspices of the West. However we have witnessed time and again that, despite China having being historically a troubled nation, its ancient civilisation has always managed to restore itself to power like a phoenix rising from the ashes.

We should not forget China is an old civilisation. Despite the rise of the Qin Dynasty in 221 BCE with its first emperor Qin Shi Huangdi, who unified under his command the disparate warring small kingdoms of the land, China already had well established mythological origins for its people and civilisation that went back some 3000 years. The Chinese often refer to themselves as the descendants of a number of deified legendary emperors of whom the most notables are the emperors Yan and Huang. Emperor Huang, referred to as the Yellow Emperor Huang di (deified form) is believed to have reigned from 2697-2598 BCE but there are no extant records in support of his physical existence. Nevertheless, on the traditional two-millennium old annual Tomb Sweeping Day Festival, also known as the Qingming Festival, when deceased ancestors are honoured by ritualised votive offerings, it has also been customary to conduct sacrificial ceremonies in remembrance of the apotheosised legendary emperors of the Chinese people.

The earliest ruling Chinese dynasty on the other hand mentioned in traditional Chinese sources is the Xia dynasty (c 2205-1766 BCE) said to have been founded by Emperor Fu Xi (Fu Hsi), son of Yu the Great, but as is the case with emperors Yan and Huang, the existence of emperors Yu and his son Fu Xi also appear to have a mythological provenance. But regardless of Xia's historical authenticity, it is abundantly clear that there were many settled communities in China scattered from west to east along the Wei and the Yellow rivers reaching all the way into the Shandong peninsula in the Bohai Bay who subscribed to these mythological anecdotes. These communities in the central plains constituted the historical heartland of ancient

China and have traditionally been known collectively as the "Middle Kingdom", the land under Heaven (tian xia).

At this point, it is hoped that it is abundantly clear to the reader what gives the Chinese a sense of what it is to be Chinese, and that it does not emanate from being a citizen of a Chinese nation but rather from being the inheritor and the future transmitter of the several thousand-year old Chinese culture and civilisation. We may contrast this with the concept of being an American, English, French or a German, which without doubt take form only from the inception of their respective nations during more recent time frames. Therefore, we may agree there was no American civilisation, as we define civilisation, prior to 1776 and indeed even at the time of the expeditions of Lewis and Clark, nor English civilisation prior to Alfred the Great in the 10th century. The point here is that Western nations derive their individualised identities from their very recent nation-state histories unlike the Chinese who draw their identities and inspirations from their deep rooted ancient civilisation.

The words of the current President of China, Xi Jin Ping, reverberate with the echoes of China's past emperors and recent leaders, and resonate with his clarion call for the 'great rejuvenation of the Chinese civilisation.' In this compact book, presented to itinerant readers, wide-ranging discussions and points of view are offered to challenge the readers' international political perceptions and to ponder their future, and the future of generations to come, shaped by the many-faceted relationships that exist between the US and its allies versus an emerging People's Republic of China. Will China ultimately accept the West's belief in the indisputable connection between democracy, economic growth and progressive social welfare, or will China in the long run stand as a model of a successful one-party dictatorial state and a beacon for others to emulate? Consider the Chinese public's approval rates of their central government's legitimacy and performance. The current attitude to their country's general direction stands at 85% approval versus a mere 26% for the democratic United States. The Chinese public's opinion that their current standard of living is higher than it was 5 years ago stands at 73% compared to US's 27%. Eighty-two percent of the Chinese believe the future holds a greater promise for the next Chinese generation as opposed to only 33% in the US; and the Chinese public's level of optimism about their future stands at a phenomenal 93%. These results are a reflection of China's practice of 'responsive authoritarianism' whereby the central government bolsters its legitimacy through constructive responsiveness to surveys collected by public opinion companies which canvas even the lowest level of the Chinese social stratum. In contrast, the West's woes remain entangled in the democratic cycles of elect-regret-elect which has become a major hindrance to social progress in the West and the root cause of the public's repeated searches for competent governance.

Although this particular paragraph does not necessarily directly address the subject of this book, it does however appropriately visit the reasons for the American social malaise raised above. Hence, we witnessed in our 2016 national elections and for the first time in American history the election of Donald J. Trump as our 45th president, a man totally outside of Washington's corridors of power and typically a businessman without any former political experience. In doing so, the American people demonstrated unequivocally their loss of faith in the competence of our traditional governing class. The voting public - the forgotten man – had decided that the arrogance of their senators, of their congressmen and state governors had become the perpetual self-enrichment tool for the elites in Washington while they have ignored and badly neglected the basic social needs of the common man. The extent of this neglect, while the governing class of Washington enjoyed a blanket of security orchestrated by their elitism, fostered the gradual division in the American population in the form of racism, social discrimination, nationalism, xenophobia and public discontent and violence. It is a long road to healing. It is hoped that re-considering the American global interests and foreign policies outside the ideology of 'American exceptionalism' may restore for the American public some semblance of proper governance and social wealth and unity.

This book is not focused exclusively on how China deals with the United States. Foreign policy agendas are also presented in relation to China's involvement and influences in Pakistan, India, Canada, Africa, the Middle East, Central Asia, Indonesia and Japan. Hopefully, the discourse on these subjects would be seen to offer a balanced view of China and its cultural traditions, and also to raise enquiring questions as to whether international conceptions about China are correct.

Jacob G. Ghazarian
Oxford, 2017

Chapter I

What History Tells Us

What and how China thinks then and now? These are indeed perplexing questions. Although they can be exemplified in the metaphoric saying of Deng Xiao Ping, the paramount political leader of the People's Republic of China in the late 1970s 'It does not matter what colour the cat is as long as it catches mice,' the truths that underpin this metaphor are considerably more complex. We will come back to Deng Xiao Ping a little later.

The 7th Century

To begin our discourse, let us go back in history and consider fleetingly the case of Wu Zetian, the concubine of Emperor Tai Zong (626-49 CE) of the Tang dynasty upon whose death Wu became first the concubine and then the wife of Tai Zong's son and successor Emperor Gao Zong (649-83 CE). She bore the emperor four sons whose rules were all masterminded by Wu until she finally usurped the throne from her youngest son Rui Zong in 690 CE. Upon declaring herself Empress of China, the dominant Confucian leaders of her court questioned the legitimacy of her action on the basis of the prevailing ethics regarding the subservient role of women in their traditional Chinese social order.[†] Wu Zetian was quick to summon the Buddhist clergy of her court and enquired if such a discriminatory dogma can be found in the tenets of Buddhism. Needless to say, the leaders were thus hopelessly out-manoeuvred. Wu Zetian was a ruthless and a cruel ruler; she spared no lives for securing her political dominance even at the expense of arranging the murder of her first son Li Zong. Likewise, in 701 CE she orchestrated the killings of her grandson Prince Yidi and of her seventeen-year-old granddaughter Yong Tai. Prince Yidi and Princess Yong Ti were the first and seventh offspring, respectively, of Wu's third son and Emperor Zhong Zong (684, 705-10 CE). Against all odds of court intrigues and of the ample practice of using poisonous substances to settle political scores, Wu defiantly ruled as First Empress of China from 690 CE until her natural death in 705 CE leaving behind a blank stone stele willing it to be inscribed with her epitaph by those who had held monumental contempt to her course of rule. Even in death she confounded her adversaries knowing full well they would fear to speak evil of the dead.

The 16th – 18th Century

The Portuguese were the first Europeans to colonise a coastal territory in China. They arrived in Guangzhou, Guangdong province by sea in 1513 CE. By 1517 they had established a monopoly on the thriving trade out of the city's harbour on

---

[†] Although dissimilar in law, it is of interest to note that the leader of the National League for Democracy Party in Burma (Myanmar), Aung San Suu Kyi, is banned from the presidency of Burma despite her sweeping victory in the Burmese 2015 elections. According to chapter 3, no 59(f) of the Burmese constitution of 2008, the president must be someone who "[he] himself, one of the parents, the spouse, one of the legitimate children or their spouses not owe allegiance to a foreign power. They shall not be subject of a foreign power or citizen of a foreign country ... [or] be persons entitled to enjoy the rights and privileges of a subject of a foreign government or citizen of a foreign country." Aung San Suu Kyi's two sons are both British citizens.

the Pearl River which remained unchallenged until the arrival of the Dutch in the early 17th century. The Portuguese and the Dutch were soon followed by the French and the British who were determined that they as newcomers would not be denied the lion's share of the lucrative Asian markets. The British East India Company, one of many European trading conglomerates called East India Company, was granted an English Royal Charter by Queen Elizabeth I on 31 December 1600 to trade particularly in the East Indies but ultimately traded mainly with the Indian sub-continent and China.

The foundations of the British East India Company were laid when Queen Elizabeth I had granted a charter on 7 January 1592 to fifty-five English merchants under the name 'Governor and Company of Merchants of London Trading into the East Indies' giving them the monopoly of trade with Venice and Ottoman Turkey. This was the beginning of the Levant Company which ultimately led to the formation of the East India Company of Britain and the advent of the British Empire in India. The company traded mostly in cotton, silk, indigo dye, saltpetre, tea and opium, but in time came to rule large swathes of India exercising military power and assuming administrative functions to the gradual exclusion of its commercial pursuits. Under the Government of India Act of 1858, the British Crown assumed direct administration of India that came to be called the British Raj. In the eighteenth century, the British East India Company was very anxious to open up the massive Chinese market to manufactured British and colonial goods but was frustrated by China's constant indifference towards the company's overtures. And when the Court of King George III of England sent Lord George Macartney to China in 1792 in behalf of the East India Company to seek the consent of Emperor Qian Long (1735-96 CE) for installing British diplomatic and trade representatives in Peking (Beijing), the Emperor was not impressed: his response sent to King George was that China was not interested in increasing its foreign trade because it required nothing from Britain. The response read further:

> We have never valued ingenious articles, nor do we have the slightest need of your country's manufactures. Therefore, O King, as regards your request to send someone to remain at the capital, while it is not in harmony with the regulations of the Celestial Empire we also feel very much that it is of no advantage to your country.

The condescending tone of this response would not have been expected but it is to be noted that in the 18th century, during the Qing dynasty, China considered itself in every respect a single self-contained superior civilisation surrounded by less sophisticated or nomadic tribal communities whose respectability were measured by the Chinese only in relation to that of the Middle Kingdom (tzong-hua), the core of the civilisation of the Chinese nation-state.[1]

The 20th Century

A more recent history of China, constructed around the Communist Revolution of the early 1940s under the leadership of Mao Tse Tung, may give us a glimpse of the extent to which Chinese personalities have analysed circumstances in planning strategies for achieving their carefully calculated and projected political goals. Mao, who is now considered by the Chinese as the founding father of the People's Republic of China, just as George Washington is regarded as the founder of the United States, had given in his pre-revolutionary writings his own elaborate answers to the questions 'Who are our enemies?' and 'Who are our friends?' He believed the basic reason why all previous revolutionary struggles in China had achieved so little, if anything at all, was their failure to unite with real friends in order to vanquish the real enemies. Mao's monumental discourse on distinguishing real friends from real enemies was based on his thorough analyses of the economic status of the various Chinese social classes in China and of their respective attitudes towards a revolution. His assessment of the social classes produced five distinct groups whose accurate definitions allowed the identification of the poor peasants who played an inextricable role in the success of Mao's Communist Revolution.[2] The five groups were: the Landlords, Middle Bourgeoisie, Petty Bourgeoisie, Semi-Proletariat and, finally, the Proletariat. The first group was summarily dismissed as a potential source of revolutionary recruits because it was seen as an appendage of international bourgeoisie and a parasite of Western imperialism. The second was defined as opportunistic capitalists whose loyalties rested on whoever provided them with opportunities for profit and the protection of their class status. The third included the craftsmen, students, teachers, lower civil servants, office clerks and minor lawyers. They were perceived to remain neutral towards communism in peacetime but would support a revolution if the struggle is seen to be succeeding. Their ranks were divided into right-wing and left-wing, the former suspicious of revolutions and the latter fully supportive. The fourth, the Semi-Proletariat, included the share-holders working the farmlands and the semi-owner peasants who were perceived to be receptive to propaganda. The fifth group included the widespread poor rural masses that formed the backbone of Mao's revolutionary activities.[3]

Now let us return to Deng Xiao Ping. His proposals for the unification of China after the Cultural Revolution - which lasted from 1966 to 1976 - brought into the political arena the inconceivably unambiguously definable concept of One Country, Two Systems intended to appease international agendas and to reach agreements on the unification of the motherland. This concept ensured China's satisfaction and, most probably, may have been predicated on projected future opportunities that would give China the authority to achieve her carefully calculated objectives. Can this be true?

The One Country, Two Systems principle was a constitutional solution formulated by Deng Xiao Ping in the late 1980s. Deng put forth the proposition that there can be only One China with autonomous regions, such as Hong Kong and Macao, subordinate to the authority of Chinese Central Government in Beijing yet allowing the regions to maintain their existing domestic political systems undisturbed in order to manage their economics and financial affairs. What mattered to Beijing was the image of holding incontestable territorial sovereignty over Hong Kong and Macao. Thus, Deng's proposals formed the foundations upon which the repatriations of colonial Hong Kong and Macao became possible on 1 July 1997 and 20 December 1999 respectively.

The 21st Century

But, as early as 2002, cracks began to appear in the One Country, Two Systems stipulation concerning Hong Kong. This cast shadows of dark omens on the future internal and domestic political autonomy of the now repatriated territory. Observations by several international groups of political analysts have expressed doubt about the true intentions of the Chinese Central Government regarding Hong Kong. On 24 September 2002 the local government under Beijing's sphere of influence proposed Article 23 of the Hong Kong Basic Law, a bill to address national security. At the time of its drafting the bill was considered protective of civil rights, but it soon became clear it was designed to pre-empt political unrest. Under British rule, Hong Kong had a number of laws rarely enforced regarding national security but the implementation of Article 23 would replace the British colonial era laws and introduce new wordings on anti-subversion, treason, sedition, secession and the banning of local and foreign political organisations. However, on the heels of corruption issues and the widespread public protests that it had precipitated, it became clear that the bill would not get the necessary support from the local legislative council hence it was withdrawn indefinitely. Nevertheless, the Article 23 exercise was seen as the beginnings of an effort to undermine Hong Kong's localised autonomy and thus had shed doubts on Beijing's pledges to abide by the One Country, Two Systems framework. It is outside the scope of this book to review the details of Article 23 which can easily be found on the internet, however we can here ask: 'Was China covertly reneging on its commitments regarding the accords reached in 1997?'

Enter the Umbrella Movement of 2014, in recognition of the umbrella as a symbol of defiance. Having failed to implement Article 23 in 2002, over a decade later the Beijing's Standing Committee of the People's Congress then proposed reforms to Hong Kong's electoral system for 2016 as enshrined in Article 45 of the Hong Kong Basic Law. In its proposal, the standing committee required that a new system be developed to elect the Legislative Council via universal suffrage with the approval of Beijing and that the Chief Executive-elect of Hong Kong would have to be appointed by the Central People's Government. Pro-democracy advocates viewed Beijing's decision as a betrayal of the principle of 'one person, one vote,' in that candidates deemed unsuitable by the Beijing authorities would have been pre-emptively screened out by the proposed system. Massive spontaneous sit-in street protests were the response, demonstrated mostly by the Hong Kong Federation of Students. Their defiant demonstrations extended over a period of three months from 26 September, ending on 16 December 2014. The protests eventually ended without any political concessions from the Beijing government and triggered political assault from the mainland on academic freedoms and civil liberties of activists.

As would be expected, mainland Chinese officials and media alleged that outside 'hostile forces' fomented the protests, and accused democracy advocates of being tools for subversion by

Western forces that were set at undermining the authority of the Communist Party. The *People's Daily* wrote 'The US may enjoy the sweet taste of interfering in other countries' internal affairs, but on the issue of Hong Kong it stands little chance of overcoming the determination of the Chinese government to maintain stability and prosperity.' No doubt Beijing was very much aware that concessions in any one place may risk similar demands from China's other autonomous regions but particularly from the mostly Islamic Xinjiang province and from ethnic Tibet. It had come to light that at the height of the demonstrations, Hong Kong officials were in meetings behind closed doors with mainland officials in neighbouring Shenzhen who in turn were planning a robust strategy to deal with the protests under the direct supervision of the highest leadership in Beijing. Furthermore, the Hong Kong Federation of Students, which had been hoping to send a delegation to meet with the leadership in Beijing for concessions, was simply rebuffed and dismissed.

Let us now return to my earlier question about Hong Kong: 'Was China covertly reneging on its commitments regarding the handover accords reached in 1997? Again we must turn our attention to China's historical records to reach an acceptable consensus.

China in 221 BCE was primarily an agrarian society that focused on the production of rice, wheat and soybeans. Pigs and chickens were raised on communal farmlands where ownership and duties were shared. Whilst horses and oxen were used to plough the fields, sheep were kept mainly for the production of wool. In contrast to this agrarian environment that typified the Middle Kingdom, the peoples of the grasslands beyond the borders to the north and north-west of the Qin heartlands were primarily nomadic dwellers of open pastures referred to as 'the barbarians' who frequently raided adjacent lands in China. We note that the First Emperor of China, Qin

Shi Huangdi of the Qin Dynast had proclaimed with great self-praising modesty: 'Insignificant as I am, I have raised troops to punish the rebellious princes; and thanks to the sacred power of our ancestors all six kings have been chastised as they deserved, so that at last the empire is pacified.' Yet we find the cycle of unity and national dismemberment issues were pervasive throughout Chinese history up to 1949. No doubt, the prime objective of the 1949 communist revolution was to bring about a cohesive union of the Chinese people. Hence we can see that the direction of Chinese civilisation has been towards a singular centrally ruled society as opposed to the Western pattern of forfeiting the sovereignty of the central authority by separating sedentary populations and dividing territories, a practice that go back to the time of Emperor Diocletian. His reign is characterised as the beginning of the decline and fall of the Roman Empire. In this context, the Romans abandoned their early practice of ruling their empire by an all-powerful central government. Their inability to centrally govern a large and an extended empire was the impetus that led Emperor Diocletian to divide the Roman Empire in 285 CE (there were a number of reasons for this inability to centrally govern the Roman Empire, but fundamentally they were all linked to implementing bad laws, e.g., a person was required to own land and be a Roman citizen to qualify to serve as a Roman soldier). Despite the re-unification efforts by Emperors Constantine the Great and Julian the Apostate in the 4th century, the division of sovereign lands continued soon thereafter under Emperor Theodosius I.

The Chinese ironically had also recognised the futility of centrally governing a vast expanse of territory, like China, but they did not resort to dividing their empire into independent oligarchies. Although Emperor Qin Shi Huangdi's unification of China under his supreme authority represented a mere political achievement, the truth of the matter is far from what is assumed. Historically, China has always exercised the power of the central authority, even to our present time, by delegating that authority to regional and local subordinates – in effect the uneven division of power – to conduct the specifically laid-out business of the central authority throughout the land. The distinction in this exercise however was delegating authority to fit the local circumstances modelled on variations of the basic demands (e.g., to require tribute appropriate for the locality, the choice of the recipients of the delegated authority due to regional multicultural compositions, loyalty terms and the forms of expressing that loyalty to the state and also to what extent the locality will have the authority to trade). These considerations by definition represented varied governance systems that governed the vastness of the land and its populations throughout the history of China yet each under the yoke of the central authority which remained omniscient and strangely omnipresent. In short, large tracts of the land were autonomously ruled yet their sovereignty belonged to the central authority, the state. It is important here to realise the distinction between what is described above as autonomous rule as opposed to the autonomous rule commonly practised by a vassal in feudal medieval Europe. In the latter case the sovereignty of the feudal lands belonged to the vassal, not the state, in exchange for the vassal's pledge of fealty to the state's head, usually a king, vice-regent or a count, etc.

I include here a few examples of the bureaucratic systems put in place by the ancient Chinese dynasties for ruling China, which in fact in some form are also practised in today's China. The Qin dynasty's first emperor in 221 BCE was the first to abolish China's old feudal system and divided his unified lands into 36 provinces (34 today) and each was given an autonomous governor, an army commander and an inspector. Hence each governor was overseen by an inspector who, like the governor, owed allegiance to the state. This uneven division of bureaucratic governance limited the possibilities of large regional insurrections and rebellions. Moreover, the emperor insisted that his realm's nobility move to the capital where they could be kept under a watchful eye. But most importantly, in 214 BCE he directed massive demographic relocations to the north and south in his bid to subdue and colonise border areas. Each colonised area was also given autonomy as described above. The Han dynasty, which immediately followed the Qin, continued the bureaucratic rule it inherited from the Qin and in fact relaxed somewhat the supreme authority of the emperor. The Han began to restore and institute Confucian ethics in the conduct of governance so that the selection of civil servants throughout China in service of the state was normalized. This governance became so successful that in 141 BCE the emperor Wu di restored some limited centralized authority to avert the possibility of rebellions. Nevertheless, this was a time when free trade, subject to state taxation, began to evolve along the western frontiers of China that formed the initial aspects of the Silk Road. This pattern of governance continued to remain the paradigm of rule through China's cyclic history of unification and fragmentation. We might note that the unified periods in China were 221 BCE-200 CE [Qin and Han dynasties], 581-1279 CE [Sui, Tang and Song dynasties] and 1368-1644 CE [Ming dynasty]. In contrast the disunity periods in China prevailed from 200-581 CE [Wei, Shu, Wu, Western Jin and Northern Wei dynasties], 1279-1368 CE [Yuan dynasty], 1644-1911 CE [Qing dynasty] and 1911-1949 CE [Republican period]. The historical details of these cycles can be found in any reputable history book on China.

I should think that having digested the above information, we must come to the conclusion that the One Country, Two Systems principle formulated by Deng Xiao Ping in the late 1980s regarding the handover of Hong Kong's sovereignty was actually a legitimate workable constitutional solution which to Deng's mind must have truly represented his ability to draw strength and wisdom from the practices of his civilisation's forbearers going back for at least 2000 years. From as early as 221 BCE they ruled a vast land inhabited by multicultural populations who practised their many belief systems, free trade and commerce under the watchful eye of the state yet under the umbrella of one civilisation but different systems that were appropriately used for the appropriate sector of the empire. Hence we must step back and catch our breath for a fresh consensus on the political state of Hong Kong and Macao. Finally, we should not forget that a number of provinces within mainland China today, e.g. Xinjiang, Inner Mongolia, Tibet, Ningxia and Guangxi, are designated autonomous regions that for decades have worked alongside the state for their mutual benefit.

Chapter II

Points of View

China asserts that human rights and personal liberties are not inherent in her Confucian[†] social values anchored on the notions of filial piety and in the respect of those who provide shelter and sustenance whether that is the family father or, on the grander scale, the governing state institution itself. A notable statesman who came after Confucius was Shang Yang (390–338 BCE)

---

† Kong Fu Zi, otherwise known in the West as Confucius (551-479 BCE), was a scholar and a social philosopher who lived during the Eastern Zhou dynastic rule (772-481 BCE). His commentaries on the Chinese literary classics and personal morality in politics (The Analects) developed into a pragmatic philosophy which defined ideas on discipline, social morality and respect. In the main, the Confucian philosophy, or Confucianism, described a state ideology which by far incorporated the most sophisticated ethical doctrines in a bureaucratic system of governance. It advocated two institutions: one was government and the other the family. The elements of the former described the exclusion of the masses from governmental decision-making process as a positive virtue allowing the officials to function in their capacity in keeping with the ethics and ideals with which they have been inculcated. Hence the [State] has consistently been seen as the apogee of the Chinese social order enjoying sovereignty over all national decisions - as opposed to the European models in which the power of governments has always historically been subject to competing sources of authority, such as the Church, special interest groups and lobbyists. Confucianism's family precepts are anchored on the notion of filial piety which advocates respect of fatherly authority within a family unit, or on a larger scale, the ruling State - the keeper and the vigilant protector of the ancient Chinese civilization.

of the Xianbei's Qin state. He strongly advocated Confucian principles which emphasised the rule of law and considered loyalty to the state to be above that of the family. The West must fully understand, digest and assimilate this deeply rooted Chinese secular belief system with all its implied contexts that are firmly engraved in the millennia-old Chinese tradition-linked psyche before there can be any hope of anticipating a level playing field in political encounters with China. The practices of respect and personal honour within the Chinese ancient societies are millennia old and are the cornerstone of this ancient civilisation. China sees human rights as a particularly Western preoccupation to which the West claims unjustly a virtuous monopoly and aggressively defends them around the globe for its own political interests. We are reminded of the 20th century history of Western colonialism and the evils of its exploitations in Asia, Africa and Latin America. Abundant references are brought to our attention of Europe's earlier history in the 15th and 16th centuries when racial intolerances were rampant and secular as well as ecclesiastical European Christians were burning one another at the stake for heresy and sorcery in the name of their religion. Yet still, as recently as the 20th century, innocent young men and women in the West suffered in silence and were abused or even imprisoned as in England for their sexual proclivities. Is it not appropriate therefore to say that those who live in glass houses should refrain from throwing stones on others? Hypocrisy should be exercised with caution. These are points well taken and should give the West cause to pause, probe and interrogate its ethos and re-visit its commitments to humanism. Referring to the issue of human rights, President Xi has called for all countries to continually improve their protection of human rights; and has added 'China attaches great importance to human rights. We have found a path suited to China's conditions.'

It seems, therefore, that we often condemn China's political system for its violations of the human rights of Chinese citizens and thus allow the world to perceive Chinese rule as being singularly authoritarian and oppressive. Yet, unlike our full appreciation of the precepts of Western democracy, we have little comprehension of the cultural ethos of the Chinese society, or of its Asian counterparts, and the historical elements that have shaped their fundamentals. In the world at large, especially in the Near East where the West's economic interests are paramount, there are familiar dynastic societies ruled by monarchs; there are others that govern themselves under the practice of tribal loyalties, and still more whose governments are influenced or overtly ruled by fundamentalist clerics or driven with the zeal of nationalism. Many of these societies ignore or at best pay lip service to human rights issues. Admittedly, they are allowed to escape our condemnation and even our tacit disapprovals. It behoves us, therefore, to delve deeply into 'Orientalism'† in order better to comprehend the root causes of the contemporary social unrests confronting modern China, and, most importantly, to consider whether the 'native' Chinese populace, or indeed the Japanese and other Asians, can perceive their existence in a non-Confucian non-hierarchal nation-state where the Christian concept of sinning bears no temporal or spiritual significance, but public shame is a matter of life and death.

Before we embark on a journey to explore the roots of perceived age-old sociopolitical characteristics of the Chinese populace, and to what extent they are shaped by historical circumstances in which China was often a victim, it is worth visiting Mark Leonard's description of an aspect of Chinese cultural practice which adds substance and meaning to the present discourse. He writes that the Chinese employ:

---

† Orientalism is knowledge or customs specific to Asian culture, people or language and often used in reference to a patronizing Western attitude towards Middle Eastern, Asian and North African societies. These societies are unfortunately depicted by the West as static and undeveloped as opposed to that of Western societies as developed, rational, flexible, and superior.[1]

a well-worn strategy designed to bewilder and co-opt outsiders. We spent many hours engaged in polite conversation without touching on the specifics of our co-operation. These elaborate courtship rituals, seemingly devoid of substance or direction, have been honed over centuries to nullify Western negotiating strategies and bind foreigners into Chinese ways of doing things, creating webs based on personal contact rather than contractual obligations… …..But after spending what felt like weeks in these introductory meetings, sitting around sipping tea and exchanging pleasantries, I ended up getting sucked in.[2]

In his most informative accounts of his experiences while in China over a period of several years, Mark Leonard concludes that while the West primarily views China in the current world order in economic, political or military terms, China nonetheless should be considered a fermenting powerhouse replete with political and pragmatic ideas that could challenge and ultimately influence the order of our world. A fundamental aspect of this challenge rests in China's economic successes repeated over many decades which have nullified and undermined the West's belief in the indisputable connection between democracy, economic growth and progressive social welfare. Thus China may in the long run stand as a model of successful one-party dictatorial state and a beacon for others to emulate. No doubt the strength of this model is bolstered by the debates within groups of select Chinese intellectuals frequenting the hallowed corridors of power in Beijing who have abandoned China's old political ideas based on foreign models and are forging ahead with their own non-Western independent perceptions of governance.

Chapter III

The Militarists

Our journey exploring the roots of perceived age-old socio-political characteristics of the Chinese populace must necessarily begin with China's ancient history - a history of dynastic conflicts, repeatedly fractured national unity, obsessive attempts to hold a nation together and not least the humiliating ordeals of foreign occupations. For our present purposes we will not delve into the modern Chinese history whose origins may be traced to 1921 CE when the Chinese Communist Party was founded under Mao Tse Tung. In contrast, the ancient history of China spans several millennia beginning in 2205 BCE with mythological founders of the Chinese civilisation and ending with the demise of the Qing dynasty a decade after the failed Boxer Uprising in Shandong province in 1901 CE at the hands of a European alliance. The history of the intervening years is briefly summarised in Table I below. The dynastic periods identified in the table as *Spring and Autumn* and *Warring States* derive their names from dynastic chronicles. The designation Spring and Autumn period is derived from the *Spring and Autumn Annals* of the state of Lu. The state was situated in the central and south-western regions of Shandong province and was a vassal state of the Western Zhou dynasty but rose to prominence during the Eastern Zhou dynasty. It chronicled their extant political circumstances but also included in their annals the chronological history of the inclusive years of the first half of the Eastern Zhou period. Similarly, the designation Warring States period is derived from the *Record of the Warring States* period which is a historical chronicle compiled early during the Han dynasty and represents the history of the second half of the Eastern Zhou period.

As for the tribes mentioned in Table I, it should be noted that the Xianbei Tuoba and the Xiongnu were Mongolic nomadic tribes that periodically harassed China across its northern and north-western frontiers. Late in the 4th century the Xianbei Tuoba tribe unified the many of the northern steppe tribes and founded the Northern Wei dynasty. The Tangut, on the other hand, were western nomads regarded mostly as Tibetan in origin who lived in parts of present-day Yunnan, Gansu Sichuan and Ningxia provinces. The Quan Rong are classified as a nomadic tribe of the Qiang tribe whose ancestral origins are linked to the Tangut of Tibet.

From a cursory review of the record given in Table I, especially for the periods involving the incursions by the nomadic tribes Quan Rong, Xiongnu, and the Xianbei Tuoba, it becomes abundantly clear that throughout Chinese history concerted efforts were made by China's ruling dynasties to enjoin their fragmented homeland and maintain a national unity. Despite such efforts, the first, second and the third Chinese empires were dismantled either by forces from within China, by those acting from the surrounding territories or, ultimately, by foreign forces that represented European commercial interests. It is not difficult therefore to understand the enduring Chinese obsession with maintaining social order, territorial integrity and national sovereignty.

Many of the age-old socio-political characteristics of the Chinese populace in a historical context stem undoubtedly and decidedly from home-grown principles unlike those practiced throughout European history. There have been many Chinese historical militarists who in their writings have advocated and described their models on the use of deception as a means to perception management in all manners of political and military statecraft. Their ranks include Sun Tzu, Sun Bin (or Pin) and many others (see Table II). Furthermore, a more comprehensive definition of the term deception in the present usage may include manipulation, scheming and mystification.

The most notable militarist is Sun Tzu. He was born during the Wu dynasty in the late Spring and Autumn period (c.544–496 BCE). He is well known as the author of *The Art of War* which describes managing conflicts and winning battles.[1] In his treatise on the art of war, apart from his elaborate descriptions of military strategies and plans, Sun Tzu remarks on the merits of a general as one who is able to confound the enemy: 'Hence that general is skilful in attack whose opponent does not know what to defend; and he is skilful in defence whose opponent does not know what to attack.' Furthermore, his approach to military conflicts does not necessarily place the use of force as the fundamental element in warfare, but advocates that victory is inextricably linked to psychological dominance and exploitation of the enemy's weaknesses. One way to achieve psychological dominance is the use of deception with the explicit objective being the disruption of the condition of harmony that exists between the enemy's leadership and its society and instead create a condition rampant with chaos, dilemmas, mistrusts, uncertainties and confusions as Sun Tzu writes: 'The supreme art of war is to subdue the enemy without fighting' or 'If you are far from the enemy, make him believe you are near.' In the arsenal of deceptions Sun Tzu includes harming enemy morale by breaking or shifting alliances and evading battle altogether when it is most anticipated. In our modern times such considerations may also include covert diplomacy and the public information media.

A descendant of Sun Tzu was Sun Bin (c.380-316 BCE) who served as a military strategist in the State of Qi during the Warring States period and promulgated his ancestral logics on military conflicts. In this context we may note the factual exemplary story of Sun Bin's advice to his king, Wei, of the State of Qi as to whether the king should aid the State of Han against their formidable enemy, the State of Wei, which was posed for war. His first advice was to promise aid to the Han as that would encourage their soldiers to fight with added vigour. On the second day of the planned battle as Qí's promised aid-army moved into position, Sun's second advice was that the Qí forces would light 100,000 cooking camp fires in their encampments fuelled with animal flesh and fat to fill the air with smells of plenty. On the third day, the number of camp fires was to be reduced to 50,000 and on the fourth day reduced further to 20,000. From the first fires the Wei generals initially feared the number of combined Han-Qí forces facing them, but as the surprisingly large number of fires dropped off, the apparent desertion among the enemy's ranks as assumed by the Wei forces was taken as evidence of Wei's stereotypic prejudices of their enemy's fickleness and disloyalties. However, Wei's ensuing confidently undisciplined and disarrayed attack ended in defeat as they entered a narrow gorge planned by the Han-Qi forces as a place for ambush.

Table II shows how Chinese militaristic traditions have been systematically perpetuated and practiced over the centuries from as early as the 11th century BCE. Even as late as the 20th century, the precepts of *The Art of War* were put into action in the communist revolutionary struggles under the leadership of Mao Tse Tung. The retreats during his army's 'Long March' from the province of Hunan to Yan'an in Shaanxi province were riddled with diversions to avoid or confound the nationalist forces, and were executed with small surprise attacks on nationalist fortification as screens for the strategic retreats. Many of the tribal warlords in the western regions of China were hostile to the communists as well as the nationalists and preferred to save their forces. But Mao's relentless efforts ultimately secured the alliances of the Yi people of Guizhou, Sichuan and Yunnan provinces which facilitated the safe passage of the Red Army in its strategic retreats. These manoeuvres by the Red Army are no doubt examples of strategies described in *The Art of War* skilfully implemented by Mao and his communist revolutionaries in pursuit of victory.

Stratagem

From the above collective discussions concerning Chinese historical militarists approach to deception, the term 'stratagem' has been introduced to represent this valued aspect of Chinese cultural heritage. Stratagem hence encompasses the means of perception management, forging or breaking alliances, avoiding confrontation, manipulation of the enemy and mystification. The latter term is taken to mean to perplex by playing upon the credulity of a person – that is his gullibility, his willingness to believe or trust too readily. Although the application of stratagem as statecraft or its use in warfare is not necessarily unique to China, the historically demonstrated use of stratagem, and especially the abundant attention given to it in Chinese recorded warfare literature, has led Western foreign policy makers and scholars to identify stratagem broadly with China. However, we must not be misled into thinking that stratagem is manifested exclusively in warfare. Since warfare in essence is a form of competition for supremacy, it follows that all forms of competition by necessity require the application of stratagem for achieving a specific objective; hence it may span equally both in wartime and peacetime. But, with our focus on China and its traditions, perhaps areas of economics, foreign affairs or even international sports in which China is an opponent might be suitable topics for our further considerations in the present context.

TABLE I: Ancient Dynasties of China

Dynasty	Period	Capital	Record
Shang	c1600-1027 BCE	Anyang;	Wu Ding marries Fu Hao in alliance with nomadic tribes.
Western Zhou (Xi)	1027-771 BCE	Xi'an	From Wei river valley; usurped power from Shang.
Eastern Zhou	772-221 BCE	Luoyang	King Ping moves capital in 770 BCE due to Quanrong attacks.
Spring and Autumn	772-481 BCE		Represents first half of Eastern Zhou period. Ji(s) of the State of Lu in Shandong becomes one of the smaller Warring States.
Warring States	475-221 BCE		Represents second half of Eastern Zhou period; the rise of the seven warring states.
Qin	221-206 BCE	Xi'an	Qin tribe triumphs, Ying Zheng unifies the land as the First Empire and himself the First Emperor; China's political infrastructure changes for the first time from fiefdoms to a bureaucratic system.
Han (Western)	BCE 206-8 CE	Xi'an	Liu Bang relaxes his supreme authority and restores Confucian ideology; Emperor Wudi sends Zhang Qian west seeking alliances against the nomadic Xiongnu; the roads travelled by Qian formed the earliest thoroughfares of the 'Silk Road'; established military post to secure flow of trade.
Han (Eastern)	25-220 CE	Luoyang	Fragmentation to the Three Kingdoms; Wei clan emerges but overcome by the Jin.
Western Jin	265-316 CE	Luoyang	Struggles to contain the incursions by nomadic tribes from the north.

Eastern Jin	317-420 CE	Nanjing	Xianbei Tuoba founds the Yan, Western Qin and Northern Wei dynasties; Tangut tribes occupies present-day Ningxia, Gansu and Shaanxi.
Sui	581-618 CE	Xi'an	Yang Jian consolidates the land into one unified nation; puts in place structured administrative government; successor Yangdi constructs the Grand Canal that linked Beijing with Hangzhou.
Tang	618-907 CE	Xi'an	The Second Empire; height of cultural sophistication; allows foreign religions to flourish; notable poets Li Bo, Wang Wei, Du Fu, Po Chu Yi; Emperor Taizong expands economic base to India, Central Asia, Japan and Korea; Tang legal code and Chinese pictographs are exported to Korea and Japan; the emergence of Empress Wu Zetian, Emperor Xuangzong, his affair with Yang Guifei and the An Lushan rebellion; withdrawal of troops from the western frontiers leading to Tibetan control of Tarim Basin; separatist tendencies of military commanders sets into motion the return to fragmentation.
Song (Northern)	960-1127 CE	Kaifeng	The Third Empire. curbs the power of regional commanders; paper money is printed for the first time; porcelain gaines ascendancy in the export market; peace with northern tribes achieved by appeasements and economic incentives.

Song (Southern)	1127-1279 CE	Hangzhou	Emperor Huizong moves the capital to Hangzhou; The Jurchen of Manchuria founds the Northern Jin dynasty; Genghis Khan overruns the Jurchen and the Song.
Yuan	1279-1368 CE	Beijing	Prevents the assimilation of the ruling minority Mongols with the native Chinese; adopts Chinese bureaucratic system of governance; trading charters are issued to Venetian and Genoese merchants; royal members are proselytized by the Nestorian Christians.
Ming	1368-1644 CE	Nanjing	Building of the Great Wall; Admiral Zheng He sails to the eastern shores of Africa and Arabia; arrival of the Portuguese and the Dutch; legal trade was restricted to Guangzhou; social unrest leads to Emperor Chuang Lieh's suicide; the State power surrendered to the Manchu.

| Qing (Manchu) | 1644-1911 CE | Beijing | The Manchurian rule is blighted by trade agreements forced upon them by the West; opium import banned and trade embargos placed on European goods; First Opium War 1839; Britain declares the island of Hong Kong crown colony under the Treaty of Nanjing of 1842 ; Second Opium War 1857; the Tianjin Treaty of 1858 exempts foreign trade from Chinese laws; Western missionaries allowed free access to the interior of China; Britain acquires the territory of Kowloon under the Treaty of Peking of 1860; Muslim secessionist movements in Yunnan, Gansu and Xinjiang (1855-73); France ends Vietnam as Chinese colony in 1884; Sino- Japanese war of 1894 gives the island of Formosa (Taiwan) to Japan under the Shimonoseki Treaty; Britain acquires the New Territories in 1898; China divided into zones managed by British, German, French and Russian legations in Peking; the Boxer Uprising of 1901. |

TABLE II

Title	Author	Dynasty	Date	Notes
Century BCE				
Six Secret Strategic Teachings[2]	Jiang Ziya	Zhou	11th	Ways to engage in war.
The Methods of the Sima[3]	Sima Rangju	Warring States	4th	Organization and strategy, State of Qin.
Wei Liaozi[4]	Wei Liao	Warring States	4th	Civil and military approach to conflict resolution, State of Qin.
Three Strategies of Huang Shigong[5]	?	Warring States	?	
Century CE				
Dialogues with Taizong[4]	Li Jing	Tang	7th	Military strategy.
Wujing Zongyao[6]	Zeng Gongliang	Northern Song	11th	Naval and land strategies.
The General's Garden[7]	Zhuge Liang	Song	12th	Plagiarized from earlier textas.
Huolongjing[8]	Jiao Yu/	Ming	14th	Gunpowder in land and naval mines.
Jixiao Xinshu[9]	Qi Jiguang	Ming	16th	Armed and unarmed fighting.

Chapter IV

Economic Perceptions

China was the world's largest economy for eighteen centuries and by all measures will be again by the end of the 21st century. It is perhaps inaccurate to describe the current Chinese economy as an emerging economy – as are the economies of Indian subcontinent and Africa - but rather an economy that is restoring its former strength and dominance. Since the 1980s the West has enthusiastically helped and supported all manners of Chinese economic reforms in anticipation of a more affluent society that would reject communism and bring about political reforms under the economic auspices of the West. However history has shown time and again that, despite it being repeatedly a fragmented nation, China has always managed to restore itself to power like a phoenix rising from the ashes.

In the late 1800s the United States, Great Britain and other European allies failed to see the relevance of colonising the entire Chinese mainland on the basis that it was too large and mostly a primitive agrarian rural environment of no potential economic advantages to the West. Hence, following the Sino-Japanese war of 1894 when China sustained a devastating destruction of its Weihai naval base in Shandong province, the West chose to annex only coastal cities in the form of free economic and trade zones immune to the extant Chinese laws regulating commerce. These annexations included Qingdao by Germany, Weihai and Shanghai by Great Britain, Dalian by Russia and Guangzhou by France. But the West's most anxiously anticipated political reforms in China over the last few decades have evaporated like a morning mist in the heat of a rising sun. China's return to world prominence began with the use of the term stratagem in her definitions of economic terms and concepts. Putting these terms into practice was perhaps designed to yield the gradual restoration of China to its former glory.

Socialist Market Economy

In pursuit of answers to China's rise, again we must consider the thoughts expressed by Deng Xiao Ping in 1979 regarding China's economic roadmap. In order to incorporate a market economy into a socialist planned economy, Deng defined his Chinese communist party's planned economy as follows: 'Of course, we do not want capitalism, but neither do we want to be poor under socialism. We believe that socialism is superior to capitalism. No, we will not take the capitalist road. The bourgeoisie no longer exist in China. We cannot say our planned economy is capitalism; it is in the primary position; it integrates with the market economy but this is a socialist market economy. The state-owned sector and the collectively owned sector are still the mainstay of our economy. Although foreign investment, which belongs to the capitalist economy, occupies a place in our economy it accounts for only a small portion of it and thus will not change China's social system.'[1]

Despite China's official definition of its economy as socialism, most Western economic analysts designate the Chinese economy clearly and without confusion as capitalism in a form where only one institution, in this case the state, has a full and total monopoly on setting its domestic and foreign rules of trade. It should not escape our attention that this model is not dissimilar to the fully capitalist objectives of a Western monopoly with the exception that there might be several players in the Western economic model as opposed to a single player in the Chinese model. The current Chinese economic powerhouse certainly does not conform strictly to the tenets of a socialist economy in which its planned productions of goods and services are for domestic consumption rather than for export and profits; where its proletariat is in control of the surplus commodities as opposed to where everyone presently in China is trying to grab his share of the abundant profits. The disfranchisement of China's working class, the increased rate of privatisation of state-owned enterprises with profits distributed to managers in the form of excessively high salaries have contributed to the great divide in social inequality with those at the pinnacle of the divide growing in size and political power. Undoubtedly this begs drawing the inescapable parallel with the current American popular concerns over its growing number of groups of elite capitalist financiers who dictate and fund the creation of domestic and foreign policies that disregard the welfare of the people and instead serve exclusively their profit-minded interests. The perceived socialist market economy of China initially constructed as state-planned monopoly has quietly evolved over recent decades into a multitude of privately owned giant enterprises (real estate, banking, transport, manufacturing, construction, etc.) that can rival in wealth and power their counterparts in any large Western city. The evidence is clear; China's gross domestic product (GDP) rose from US$ 217 billion in 1978 to more than US$ 11 trillion in 2015, and the private sector's share of the GDP per capita rose from US$ 227 in 1978 to US$ 8,280 in 2015.[2]

On the worldwide web's 'openDemocracy' site of 9 March 2010 Andy Yee in his article 'China and the West: the hedgehog's dilemma,' has described Chinese culture, in its modern form, as 'sheep-like materialistic and insensitive.' It caters unconditionally to the individual's or corporatist's sense of 'Me-ism' in all areas of profit-making and is often in cahoots with the central authorities' disregard of employee welfare, fairness and claims. Do these current Chinese social insensitivities differ significantly from those well-established capitalist economies throughout the world where, in some, even child labour exploitation and lack of employee freedoms in the name of profits are tantamount to violation of human rights? In the West we pride ourselves on the provision of free elementary and secondary education for our young children, yet in China school fees place inordinate responsibilities and financial pressures on parents who strive to have their children educated. In most Western societies some form of either free or partially free healthcare services are provided to their citizens, a condition that can readily be seen as bordering on socialism, yet in China covering an ordinary individual's healthcare costs is a dark personal dilemma despite the central government's consideration in 2009 of a state insurance scheme to expand healthcare coverage.[3]

One unique but tragic example that highlights the plight of the average Chinese citizens' lack of supportive healthcare coverage is the case of Yuan Long Hua, a migrant worker from Yunnan province employed by CQC Group. While at work on 1 August 2015 in a factory in Quanzhou, Fujian province, he accidentally fell into a vat of boiling slurry. Although he survived the horrific and unthinkable ordeal, nonetheless he had sustained 99% burns to his body. Despite the fact that some medical care payments were made by his employer, still Long Hua owed C¥ 90,000 (~US$ 14,000) for the palliative care he received from the staff of Quanzhou hospital No.180 which in October had halted treatment until the debt was paid in full. In desperation, Long Hua's relatives had managed to raise C¥ 30,000 (~US$ 4,600) so that treatment could continue; however the company was reluctant to provide further financial assistance, and furthermore had suggested that Long Hua should take his own life.

Housing and unemployment benefits are the accepted norms in our Western culture, managed through our collective tax-paying public and provided to the poor, to the unemployable and to those less able to fend for themselves, yet none of these protective social provisions exists significantly in today's China. One final comparative remark on Chinese 'socialism' will suffice to highlight our purpose herein, and that is the immediate eviction of a tenant from his abode enforced by the local police in the event the amount of rents due exceed the security deposits held in escrow by the landlord. Although this might be construed as an aspect of human rights violations, nevertheless, its implications of money-grabbing capitalist mentality at individual or corporate level cannot be lightly dismissed. In a comparable Western scenario the event would require time-consuming extended application of due process of law involving lawyers and court judgments while all along the rights of a tenant to remain in his abode are maintained to the bitter end. Perhaps no further elaboration is necessary on Deng Xiao Ping's intended meaning in his definition of 'socialist market economy.'

A Monolithic Authoritarian State?

The West, no doubt, still labels China as a monolithic authoritarian state. However, the political system in China is best described as a localised democracy centrally controlled by the Chinese Communist Party which portions the extent to which that democracy is exercised. Thus the current Chinese system has created deliberate space for loopholes in the laws that permit private bargaining and allow the state to retreat from the economy where such a retreat is in the interest of the nation and seen to take place at the behest of the Party.

Chapter IV

In this atmosphere of 'tolerated democracy' local governments have been able to pursue their own initiatives and often in defiance of the central directives. Consequently, tensions have been created between local authorities and their constituents resulting in rampant corruption charges. But, we ought to be cognizant of the market forces in the world economy, the needs of a civil society and of its dissident components, the environment and the international human rights values defined by the global community all of which, collectively, the Chinese state must ultimately deal with to forge a new relationship with its people for the better.

Although efforts are made in this book to show how a Leninist Communist China has modified its core ideology and embraced a semi-capitalist economy, the greatest surprise however is that its has also emerged with a great promise to lead a future world. There is no doubt China's Communist Party has been able to deliver over the last quarter of a century a stable political foundation and institutional support for its country's globally surging successful economy. The continued growth and success of this economy surely must remain paramount in the minds of its proponents who have partially abandoned the Leninist political ideas and pursued their own non-Western independent perceptions of governance. In the final analysis, it must bear heavily on the minds of the Party's leadership that the failure of the political path they have chosen to follow will undoubtedly spell the end of the Party and drive the nation imminently to chaos and to unavoidable fragmentation. Therefore, the necessity of a stable, strong and a dominant party leadership is pivotal for avoiding the repeats of China's history.

President Xi Jin Ping

With an endearing face notably associated with saints, the Chinese Communist Party's President Xi Jin Ping stands tall and confident alongside world leaders. Since Deng Xiao Ping came to power in the 1970s, his Party had remained faithful to the virtues of collective leadership by which political responsibilities were shared. However, Xi Jin Ping has unilaterally abandoned this practice and has systematically begun to dismantle this system of collective leadership. Since becoming military chief and general secretary of the Communist Party in November 2012 and president four months later in March 2013, Xi Jin Ping has made it abundantly clear that he singularly rules the nation and has, to the amazement of many, acquired from the Chinese populous the endearing nickname 'Xi Dada' - Uncle Xi - and used by the media. It is clear Xi Jin Ping is tightening his hold on the national power, though unlike a capricious tyrant. Nevertheless he now personally supervises the government reforms, finances, and the massive undertaking of the military reform and domestic security. In the context of domestic security, Zhou Yong Kang, a retired member of the Politburo's Standing Committee, who was in charge of the police and law enforcement infrastructure, is now being investigated for corruption. Considering the pace with which Xi Jin Ping has brought profound shifts in the nature of Chinese politics, we may ask: How is this possible for a man who for all appearances is the embodiment of a magnanimous leader?

A brief biographical sketch of Xi Jin Ping may help the reader to assess the strengths and weaknesses in the personality of this world leader who was born on 15 June 1953. His father, Xi Zhong Xun was a member of Mao Tse Tung's revolutionary army but was purged and incarcerated in 1968 during the Cultural Revolution. In the absence of his father, Xi Jing Ping at the age of sixteen followed Mao's movement and joined a farming collective group in Shaanxi province where he eventually became Party branch secretary of the production team. He joined the Communist Youth League in 1971 and the Communist Party of China in 1974. From 1975 to 1979, Xi studied chemical engineering at Beijing's prestigious Tsing Hua

University. After serving in various capacities as a junior member of the communist party, his most valuable experience came in 1985 when he was selected as part of a Chinese delegation sent to Muscatine, Iowa, to study American agriculture. There he stayed with an American family that created for him the opportunity to formulate his views on the United States. During his political career from 1982 to 2007, Xi served in three provinces, Hebei (1982–1985), Fujian (1985–2002), Zhejiang (2002–2007) and the municipality of Shanghai that included several posts in Fuzhou's (capital of Fujian province) Municipal Party Committee, then Vice Governor of Fujian and ultimately as Governor of Fujian.

In October 2007 Xi Jin Ping was appointed to the nine-man Politburo Standing Committee which was followed in March 2008 by his election as Vice-President of the People's Republic of China. For the next four years he undertook a relentless series of foreign travels visiting Mexico, Jamaica, Colombia Venezuela, Brazil and Malta to promote Chinese friendship and economic ties with the region. The pinnacle of his political successes came on 15 November 2012 when Xi Jin Ping was elected to the post of General Secretary of the Communist Party and Chairman of the Chinese Communist Party Central Military Commission making him in effect the paramount leader. As a prologue to tightening his grip on the power of the Party's elite, Xi led the new membership of the Politburo's Standing Committee and reduced its number of seats from nine to seven, with only himself and Li Ke Qiang retaining their seats from the previous Standing Committee; the remaining members were new.

Shortly after his ascension to power, President Xi's first major undertakings were fighting domestic corruption and rooting out high-ranking officials and ordinary party functionaries who had abused their authority for amassing personal wealth. Notable amongst those who have fallen victim to Xi's purge include, as noted earlier, the retired member of the Politburo's Standing Committee and the nation's security chief, Zhou Yong Kang, and more recently the life imprisonment of Bo Xi Lai, the party chief of Chongqing, the only inland municipality in south-west China. Although his restrains on the public, such as tightened controls on online social networks, suppression of political dissent and the rounding of political activists, resonate familiarity with the rule of capricious tyrants, Xi, on the contrary, is seen as being on the side of the common man as demonstrated by his unannounced appearance at a small Beijing restaurant for lunch with only one person accompanying him. He paid for the meal himself and dined with regular patrons. Clearly, he models himself as a leader who disdains extravagance and prefers to compares himself to Deng Xiao Ping. It is no wonder that Xi has gained the nickname Xi Dada.

There is no doubt Chinese sense of nationalism and national pride have attracted international attention and Xi Jing Ping, no less, a champion extolling Confucianism. Quoting Confucius, Xi has said 'He who rules by virtue is like the North Star; it maintains its place, and the multitude of stars pay homage.' In Shandong, the Birthplace of Confucius, Xi told scholars that while the West was suffering a 'crisis of confidence, the Communist Party had been the loyal inheritor and promoter of China's outstanding traditional culture.'

Although Xi has called for a decrease in the use of force preferring dialogue and consultation to solve current issues, he nonetheless on 21 May 2014, addressing a regional conference in Shanghai, called on Asian countries to unite and forge a way together, rather than get involved with third party powers. 'Matters in Asia ultimately must be taken care of by Asians. Asia's problems ultimately must be resolved by Asians and Asia's security ultimately must be protected by Asians.' Is Xi calling for a 'United Asian Federation' perhaps analogous to the European

Union? And, if so, with Xi's newly cultivated stronger relations with Russia, to what extent would this federation pose a threat to the US hegemony?

The dichotomy in the ideas explored here is highlighted by the most recent news concerning the South China Sea. According to China's official Xin Hua news agency, the US navy's Admiral John Richardson was told by Wu Sheng Li 'We will never stop our construction on the Nansha Islands.' Wu Sheng Li is the commander of the navy of the People's Liberation Army. Nansha Islands is China's name for the Spratly Islands, where Beijing is rapidly constructing the reef-like islands into facilities capable of military use. Mr. Wu has made China's confident position clear:

> The Nansha Islands are China's inherent territory, and our necessary construction on the islands is reasonable, justified and lawful. Any attempt to force China to give in through flexing military muscles will only have the opposite effect.

Chapter V

Foreign Affairs

No doubt throughout recorded human history political intrigues and deceptions have been described as the mainstay tool applied in domestic or international relations for securing varied forms of authoritative advantages. Such advantages have ranged from a localised domination of a royal court to a military supremacy in field of battle. In the latter case a good example was the Sun Bin's military advice described in the previous section, but in more recent history we may cite the aerial supremacy that the allied forces gained against the German Third Reich during World War II in the Battle of Britain. To make up numbers on the ground, a large number of bogus full-size fighter aircraft replicas were constructed by the allies and parked in takeoff formations on clearly seen runways just off the White Cliffs of Dover in England. This perception management was simply a manoeuvre by the allies in an effort to lure the German Luftwaffe into bombing sites that did not add the slightest advantage to the German military objectives while discharging their ordnances at a disadvantage. But with our present subject in mind, there are many more recent examples that can be delineated upon concerning perception management in peacetime foreign relations negotiations between China and several democracies where observers and analysts have argued as to whether the use of stratagem has been a feature of China's diplomatic agendas. Here, for example, we may consider cases involving the United States, Canada, India and Pakistan.

By way of introduction to this section, let us consider China's fairly recent public communications regarding its strategic agendas. In a broadcast of 'Dialogue' on China Central Television (CCTV) in January 2016, two eminent interviewees were questioned on various aspects of China's current military five-year plan of reforms and modernisation of its People's Liberation Army (PLA) that are expected to be complete by the year 2020. The politically most sensitive question posed by the moderator to the interviewees was the reason behind China's construction of a second aircraft carrier (the first carrier Liaoning was commissioned for service in 2012). One interviewee, representing the offices of a certain branch of the government's military arm, stated that the carrier will be used for the purposes of 'training all future pilots in landing and taking-off practices.' Some minutes later after having discussed other points concerning the reforms, the second interviewee, a retired general from one of government's military academies, inadvertently offered his opinion on the need for the second carrier by saying that 'it is to be the second of five carriers planned to be in operation by the year 2020 at which time China will be in a position to [fight any war].' Was the first interviewee unaware of his government's naval intentions? Was the second interviewee's answer to be taken as a warning to the West? Why were these conflicting opinions aired so blatantly despite the central governments strict scrutiny and censorship of all things broadcasted? Yet China's current president, who is chief of China's Communist Party and head of the military, has described the reforms as 'a major policy decision for realising the Chinese dream of a strong army.' The Global Times, a daily tabloid with a strong pro-government slant and published in China under the auspices of the People's Daily newspaper, underscores the president's remark with its own communist Chinese perspectives by affirming that 'with a strong army, China can be more politically appealing, influential and persuasive. If China has a big gap with the US in terms of military prowess, this will affect its international position and other countries' attitude toward China.'

Let us return to the subject of the first aircraft carrier Liaoning. When the hulls of three Soviet-era carriers were bought from the Ukraine in 1998, China denied that the largest 67,500-ton hull was to be modified for military use. In fact the state-run news agency Xin Hua reported that the hull was to be a floating casino berthed near Macao in southern China. The two smaller acquisitions were said to be converted to museums. But in 2005 it was disclosed that refitting work on the larger hull as a deployable aircraft carrier was in progress in China's major shipyard in Dalian, Liaoning province, ironically some 2,000 kilometres north of Macao. The fully refurbished carrier was finally commissioned as Liaoning and deployed for service in 2012 as China's latest addition to its navy's strength in the South China Sea. So, in effect, what was announced to be a floating casino has now been launched as a formidable part of China's growing naval power.

It is possible to elaborate further on China's naval strategic initiatives. Zhang Wen Mu, a former staff member of a Ministry of State Security centre, has stated that 'The navy is concerned with China's sea power, and sea power is concerned with China's future development.' This is most revealing as it addresses China's preoccupation with its control of the South China Sea, and also with the vulnerability of China to blockades of its sea lines of communication, especially the petroleum lifeline running through the Strait of Malacca; hence the logic and the justification for the prioritised focus on the accelerated construction of aircraft carriers as the navy's modified approach to new defence strategies. This is also consistent with China's involvement in Pakistan's Gwadar project discussed below. A further aspect of China's concerted efforts in pursuing the enlargement of its carrier fleet is the leadership's concern of China's vulnerability to military blockades along its eastern coastline on the East China Sea. First, the Ryukyu arc, a chain of seven islands stretching as an arc from the tip of southern Japan to northern Taiwan, can be used to deny China access to the wide-open Pacific Ocean's deep waters in the event the islands are fortified by adversarial forces. Secondly, the Bashi Strait is also a source of concern for China as it represents a potential barrier in the event of an international conflict with China. The strait between southern Taiwan and the northern reaches of the Philippines' Luzon Island is the gateway that connects the South China Sea to the Philippine Sea on the western edge of the Pacific Ocean. Access denial through the strait in part would complete the total encirclement of China along its entire eastern and southern offshore frontiers. It is not difficult therefore to appreciate China's current 2016 stance regarding its claims of sovereignty over a cluster of uninhabited rocks (referred to as islands) off the north-eastern tip of Taiwan called Senkaku Islands in Japan, or called Diaoyu Islands in China. For China, this is an initial step in securing its unencumbered access to the waters of the Pacific Ocean.

Relations with Pakistan

China and Pakistan have managed to maintain a strong friendship since the 1960s. It can be safely stated that Pakistan's ongoing troubled relation with the United States had opened significant opportunities for China to engage with Pakistan in a more skewed manner much in favour of China. Yet many in Pakistan consider China, unlike the US, a peaceful and a supportive neighbour. Moreover, surveys in the years 2009-2015, inclusive, have demonstrated 82-85% of the Pakistan population have a favourable view of China.[1]

Underpinning this relationship are some US$ 46 billion in Chinese investments in Pakistani projects that are part of the so-called China-Pakistan Economic Corridor. One project which is about more than simple trade, and has significant military ramifications, involves the Pakistan's city of Gwadar (or Gawadar) located at the strategically important position on the south-western coast of Pakistan's Baluchistan province where the Arabian Sea meets the Persian Gulf. China's significant investment of nearly US$ 175 million in the building of the deep-sea port at Gwadar was the beginning of China's long projected plans of establishing for its navy a series of coastal bases along the Indian Ocean, stretching from India's Bay of Bengal to the Arabian Peninsula's Gulf of Oman at the mouth of the Persian Gulf. The port was officially opened in 2007 and initially managed by a Singaporean company but by agreement the total operations of the port was officially handed over to China in 2013. Although China has insisted that the port would be used strictly for commercial purposes, there was, nonetheless, a concern in the West that China's interest in Gwadar may have rested in the port's potential as a Chinese naval base overseeing the Gulf's sea lanes for the shipments of crude-oil from Iran and Saudi Arabia. This possibility of a Chinese naval base in Gwadar would provide for China, at least in peacetime, a reasonably secure alternative land-based means for importing its oil and mineral needs, and also for accessing western markets all in the event the sea-routes through the Strait of Malacca are blocked under adversarial political circumstances. In this context, China's declared intention is to establish an oil delivery link between Gwadar and China's western-most province of Xinjiang either by way of land transportation across Pakistan leading to Xinjiang's recently built swift Karakorum Highway, or by the more likely possibility of constructing a permanent pipeline. No doubt, at least initially, China is able to use Gwadar as a semi-permanent facility for fuelling and provisioning naval ships - as it does elsewhere in the Indian Ocean, notably in Burma, Bangladesh, and Sri Lanka. But the inescapable truth underlying China's interest in Gwadar was clearly voiced by Pakistan's former Defence Minister Chaudhry Ahmed Mukhtar's announcement: 'We have asked our Chinese brothers to please build a naval base at Gwadar.' China needs Gwadar to project its developing naval power across the Indian Ocean and the Arabian Sea, and ultimately into the oil-rich regions of the Middle East and East Africa. Presently, China's plan to overcome its weaknesses in the Indian Ocean (for not having naval bases there) is precisely the apparent reason for its aggressive approach to building the potentially successful naval base in Gwadar. This will give China a big hand as a player in maritime diplomacy, but perhaps more significantly, opportunities to weaken or to challenge the Western domination of the World's energy resources.

China's interest in Gwadar has much 'deeper' implications. South-east Asian countries are concerned about China's geopolitical intentions because of China's accelerated annual production of submarines and the associated construction of their required bases in Hainan Island. No doubt the proximity of these bases to the many South China Sea islands over which China claims sovereignty will permit China to reinforce its objectives in the South China Sea. Some aspects of China's claims in the South China Sea are discussed in Chapter VII. The strategic intentions of China in the present context are further demonstrated first, by the docking - at least one - of its submarines in Sri Lanka's Colombo port in September of 2014; second, another submarine docking at Pakistan's port of Karachi in May 2015 and third, by finalising a deal on 19 April 2015 to sell eight submarines to Pakistan, a deal that will justify the deployment of Chinese submarines and submariners in the waters of the Arabian Sea. Although China insists its presence in these waters is to prevent the return of piracy on the open seas and maintain security, China's reliance on the credulity of the West in this instance however has not been fruitful. Nevertheless, China's intentions in long-range deployment of its navy's capabilities cannot be missed. They are to extend the arm of its striking power primarily into the Indian and the Pacific Ocean theatres.

Relations with India

The China-India border stretches over 4,000 kilometres, and China claims ownership of some 90,000 square kilometres of Indian territory that is mostly tangled up with Tibet. Large parts of India's northern mountainous regions were once part of the Tibetan Empire of the 9th century and certain other close-by regions were semi-independent kingdoms which paid tribute to the Tibetan Empire. Because Beijing since 1959 has claimed Tibet as part of China, it has, by extension, sought to claim these border areas as historically Tibetan, and therefore also belong to China.

In pursuit of these claims, China has focused its attention on India's north-eastern state of Arunachal Pradesh and of its key district of Tawang. Arunachal Pradesh borders the states of Assam and Nagaland to the south, and shares international borders with Bhutan in the west, Myanmar in the east and is separated from China in the north by the disputed McMahon Line. The apparent reason for China's focus on the state is partly because it has been a safe haven for the Tibetan spiritual leader, the Dalai Lama, as well as for his followers, and for many thousands of Tibetan exiles who live there and who seek Tibetan independence. In this context it would be natural to expect this area to be a major concern for China.

The truth behind China's concern over Arunachal Pradesh is much deeper than what meets the eye. It is not strictly confined to the fact that its districts harbour Tibetans calling for their independence but that long before China occupied Tibet in 1951, self-proclaimed independent Tibet had ceded the state to the colonial administration of British India as defined by the McMahon Line that was incorporated in the Simla/Shimla Accord of 1914. This McMahon Line is regarded by India as the legal national boundary between its state of Arunachal Pradesh and Tibet. But China rejects the Simla Accord and its McMahon Line contending that Tibet was not a sovereign state and therefore did not have the power to conclude treaties.[2] Nevertheless, Tibet's claim was that after the fall of the Qing dynasty of China in 1911, Tibet expelled all Chinese officials and troops from Tibet and declared itself independent in 1913.[3]

Indeed, early British efforts to create a boundary in this sector of Asia were triggered by their discovery in the mid-19th century that Tawang, an important trading town, was in fact in Tibetan territory. Thus, in 1873, the British-run administrative government of colonial India drew a 'Line' intended to represent part of Tibet's south-eastern international boundary.[4] This line followed the alignment of the Himalayan northern foothills, roughly the current southern boundary of Arunachal Pradesh. British maps published between 1904 and 1914 show the Tibeto-Assamese boundary lying on the Himalayan northern foothills, in conformity with the 'Line' boundary and with China's sustained insistence of Tibet's pre-1914 boundaries. However self-proclaimed independent Tibet had refused to recognise the pre-1914 British-directed boundaries thus leading to an impasse between Tibet and Britain. Fearing Russian influence interfering in this political impasse, British forces led by Sir Francis Younghusband invaded Tibet in 1904, and three years later in 1907, Britain and Russia acknowledged Chinese suzerainty[5] over Tibet. Yet, a re-drawn McMahon Line map of 24-25 March 1914 used as the basis for the Simla Accord was signed only by British and Tibetan representatives in the absence of participation by a Chinese equivalent.[6] As China continued to repudiate the Simla Accord, Tibetans considered the McMahon Line invalid until China agreed to sign the Accord.[7] Ironically, this invalidation by the Tibetans, needless to say to the delight of the Chinese, in theory at least reverts the Tibetan boundary definitions to Tibet's pre-1914 boundaries and adds much credence to the legitimacy of China's claims.

No doubt China has decided wisely to focus its claims and attention on Arunachal Pradesh because any acceptance of the 1914 Simla Accord will:
1. Amount to China's implicit acknowledgement that Tibet was once independent of China;
2. Nullify China's historical claim of suzerainty over Tibet;
3. Bestow upon Tibet the right to enter into treaties as an independent state; and most of all,
4. Ignite China's circumspectness of potential domestic uprisings by minorities within China proper struggling for secession and independence from China, for example by the Muslim Uyghur minority in Xinjiang province (a case in point but outside the scope of this writing).

The modern history of India's conflicts with the People's Republic of China begins with China's invasion of Tibet in October 1950. The origins of the conflicts stem from two issues; one involving a sector of India's northern territory called Aksai Chin, claimed by India, and another which is usually associated with the McMahon Line of a proposed map drawn in 1912 defining the boundaries between Tibet, China and British India along India's north-eastern frontier. Below we will review fairly comprehensively the fundamental aspects of these two issues but avoid the complicated and the convoluted details of the 19th century politics between Great Britain and Russia regarding the control of their respective interests in Central Asia. Such details will no doubt be outside the scope of the present discourse and not necessarily of interest to the itinerant reader.

The dispute involving the Aksai Chin territory begins in 1865 with the creation of India's northern boundary defined by the Johnson Line, which runs along the Kunlun Mountains.[8]

The line placed the territory in the eastern part of India's Kashmir region but this placement was never physically demarcated on the ground by the then government of British India. However, in 1899 British India submitted to the Chinese a modified boundary line known as the Macartney-MacDonald Line[9] that placed Aksai Chin in China but due to the extant political circumstances, the modified boundary line did not have an opportunity to be ratified by the Chinese. Hence, by the end of World War I the British officially reverted to the use of the Johnson Line and, consequently, the issue of the Aksai Chin remained unresolved. In 1947 when India acquired its independence from Great Britain, and in keeping with the official stance of the British government, independent India declared that the Johnson Line represented India's boundary with China in Kashmir and furthermore, despite poor historical evidence, it also declared that Aksai Chin had been a part of northern India for centuries. These declarations were followed in July 1954 with India's Prime Minister Jawaharlal Nehru's announcement that Aksai Chin's border as defined by the Johnson Line was non-negotiable.[10] In the final analysis, the position taken by India turned out to be a reckless and a short-sighted policy that led to the open hostilities of 1962. It has been argued, however, that the burden of the responsibility in the failure of this international diplomacy might be appropriately placed in the coercive hands of the British Empire and in the unwillingness to abandon its imperialist colonialist agendas. Nevertheless, we shall return later to these issues and discuss the manner with which the newly founded People's Republic of China implemented its intentions regarding the disputed regions of Aksai Chin and Tibet prior to the eruption of the 1962 war.

The failed diplomacy between India and China in the early decades of the 20th century concerning Aksai Chin did not become the sole source of conflict between India and China. The British Empire's concerns about potential advances of Russia unto the Tibetan plateau and into the northern frontiers of British India was the impetus that drove the empire urgently to seek and try to establish fixed boundary demarcations recognisable internationally in a region in the north-east of India, often referred to as the North East Frontier Agency (NEFA), which later became Arunachal Pradesh. Here again we find the covert diplomatic manoeuvres of the British Empire in this arena become a contributing factor to the start of the 1962 hostilities between India and China.

A report prepared in 1847 by an agent of NEFA, Major J. Jenkins, and submitted to the British government in India, defined the borders between Tibet and NEFA and also included Tawang as part of Tibetan territory. Tawang was an area in the NEFA and historically, in any event, was considered a Tibetan territory. On this basis the British government negotiated with representatives from Tibet and settled the border boundaries which remained a *de facto* border between India and Tibet. However, in 1913 representatives of Britain, Tibet and China met at the resort town of Simla/Shimla (the capital of Himachal Pradesh) to consider a proposal drawn up by the foreign secretary of the British Indian government, Henry McMahon, along the lines of Jenkins' report with a modification that returned the trading town of Tawang to British jurisdiction. The McMahon proposal came to be referred to as the McMahon Line. China did not ratify the McMahon proposal but Henry McMahon himself by-passed the Chinese and settled the border bilaterally by negotiating directly with Tibet.[11] Consequently, China took the position that Britain should not have entered into a treaty directly with Tibet in violation of the Anglo-Russian Convention of 1907, which stipulated that neither party was to negotiate with Tibet 'except through the intermediary of the Chinese government.'[12] Furthermore, China rejected Tibet's claims of independent rule. Although these boundary disputes remained in a hiatus for nearly quarter of a century, the British in the late 1930s systematically began to use the McMahon Line on their official maps of the region. The state of these disputes continued unabated even after India gained independence from Britain in 1947. But a serious decisive change in the situation came in 1950 when Tibet lost its *de facto* independence and was absorbed into the newly founded People's Republic of China under the leadership of Mao Tse Tung as President and Chairman of the Communist Party, and Zhou En Lai as Prime Minister (1949–76) and also Foreign Minister (1949–58). China justified the invasion of Tibet on the basis that it had always been a part of the Chinese motherland geographically and culturally. Some aspects of China's motives for invading and occupying Tibet will be discussed below.

Several political analysts and literary scholars have asserted that the ultimate responsibility for precipitating the 1962 war between India and China must be attributed to India's provocations of China by its occasional small skirmishes with Chinese forces on the fringes of the disputed areas as a result of India's 'Forward Policy' designed to create defensive outposts. But most importantly it was India's significant military posturing in the disputed areas that led China to assume a large scale Indian expansionist assault on Tibet was eminent hence decided to launch on 20 October 1962 simultaneous pre-emptive strikes on two separate fronts nearly 1,000 kilometres apart – a western front at Aksai Chin and an eastern front at the NEFA. On the western front, the war came to an end when China had reached its territorial claim line. On the eastern front, however, Tawang area was quickly occupied by the Chinese forces, but they voluntarily withdrew at the end of the war on 21 November 1962. Thus Tawang again came under Indian administration. But to the present day China has not relinquished its claims on most of Arunachal Pradesh including Tawang.[13]

Let us now review the manner with which China interacted with India throughout the period lasting from China's occupation of Tibet in 1950 to the beginning of the isolated skirmishes in the disputed areas that eventually precipitated the war. It seems to have been the general consensus of the international community during the time Zhou En Lai served as China's foreign minister that he methodically used procrastination and deceit in his relationship with India's Prime Minister Jawaharlal Nehru. As early as 1951-52, the government of China had indicated that there were no unresolved frontier issues that required negotiations with India. Furthermore, when Nehru in July 1954 declared that Aksai Chin's border as defined by the Johnson Line was non-negotiable, there was neither open condemnation by China nor any specific opposition to Nehru's claim. It is ironic that only two years later in November 1956 Zhou En Lai gave his assurances that China had no claims on Indian territories despite his official Chinese maps of the time had included within China's borders 90,000 square kilometres of territory claimed by India.[14] Yet, in the years just preceding the war we find Zhou En Lai arguing that since no boundaries were demarcated for the Aksai Chin by treaty between any Chinese or Indian authority, therefore Nehru's Indian government could not unilaterally define the region's borders. He further argued that since Aksai Chin was already under Chinese jurisdiction, China could accept the proposed Macartney-MacDonald Line.[15]

From a general view of these negotiations, certain conclusions have been drawn regarding China's *modus operandi* in dealing with India's Prime Minister Jawaharlal Nehru. Capitalising on Nehru's trust in his friendship with Zhou, and in his firm belief that an amicable settlement can be reached with China, it is believed that Zhou En Lai had resorted to the use of the fundamental teachings of Sun Tzu's *The Art of War*, that is, procrastinating a resolution of the conflicts with India on the basis that there were no major border disputes between them, or that his offices had not had an opportunity to revise maps the communist party had inherited from the defeated nationalist government. Furthermore, Zhou's procrastinations with great patience stretching interminably were fundamental in removing the subject of his bilateral talks with Nehru from the probing eyes of the media and the public, thus not only frustrating and demoralising the opposition, but also allowing the issues to appear less urgent and less relevant with the passage of time and ultimately cloaking the disputes from public interest. Also, in the late 1950s in all the skirmishes with Indian forces along the disputed lines, China consistently evaded and did not significantly and materially engage the Indians in battle when a major battle seemed most imminent but, instead, focused its efforts on Chinese forces' readiness to subdue the enemy at an advantageous point in time. Mystification also seemed to have been employed by Zhou. Having first-hand knowledge of Nehru's naivety and gullibility, Zhou had surmised the newly independent India's first prime minister was set on a course of achieving harmony with India's neighbours, confident in the newly emerging Asian anti-imperialist attitude which was rejuvenated by the dissolution of the British Empire.

Perhaps it might be beneficial at this point to remark briefly on the current situation regarding the border disputes between China and India. A recent quote stated that: 'China sees India as an important power from an economic and geopolitical viewpoint, and wants a better relationship with it.' However, as China's military stature has grown over the last several decades, its position on negotiating with India has been less flexible. Although China in 1913 had refused to ratify the validity of the McMahon Line in Arunachal Pradesh, we find China in 1985 proposing its recognition of Indian sovereignty over the eastern territory (Arunachal Pradesh) if India would reciprocate by acknowledging China's sovereignty over the western territory of Aksai Chin. India rejected this proposal on the grounds that Aksai Chin had always been under the jurisdiction of India hence China's proposal not only did not represent a concession, but China's continued occupation of Aksai Chin was illegal. India's position was reinforced by turn of events in subsequent years which gave rise to a significant level of doubt and distrust on the part of India regarding whether China was truly seeking a resolution of their boundary disputes rather than, again, set on a course of credulity and deceit. The reason for India's doubts stemmed from China's peculiar reaction to India's rejection. China reversed the terms of its 1985 proposal and suggested that India give up its claims in the eastern territory, hence China would retain its sovereignty over the entirety of Arunachal Pradesh in exchange for its recognition of Aksai Chin as Indian territory. What was China's objective by these bargaining strategies? The answer seems rather simple, even if partly correct. China was aware of Nehru's past dismissive remark in reference to Aksai Chin's cold desert-like environment as quoted: 'where not a blade of grass grows.' However, with China's increasing industrial demands for natural resources and energy, Arunachal Pradesh, as opposed to barren Aksai Chin, contains a wealth of resources in minerals, rare earth elements and a potential source of hydroelectric power that can be generated from the massively flowing waters of the mountainous terrain. If in the past China had focused its desire to annex Aksai Chin for national security reasons that desire seems to have been abandoned as the area is no longer relevant in 21st century China with its massive military capabilities able to rapidly react to any national threat or emergency within or across Tibet.

The current situation remains a stalemate. Indian President Pranab Mukherjee visited Arunachal Pradesh in late November 2013 and declared the area 'an integral and important part of India.' In response, China's foreign ministry issued an angry rebuttal stating 'the area is under illegal Indian occupation and China's stance on the disputed area on the eastern part of the China-India border is consistent and clear.'

While the border disputes between India and China have occupied much of the two country's geophysical interests, China has aggressively followed another path that demonstrates its quiet hostility towards India. During the past decade, India's geopolitical and military stature has been significantly improved and strengthened as a result of its close ties with the United States. Consequently, China had turned its attention to friendship with Pakistan in order to balance the intrusion by the US in the Indian subcontinent. From the beginning of this friendship, China has been Pakistan's largest weapons supplier. But more importantly, China helped Pakistan acquire the equipment and the technology required to develop its own nuclear arms. History tells us that India and Pakistan have fought three wars since 1947 and that the introduction of nuclear weapons into the Pakistan-India military theatre has subdued hostilities between them and restricted their conflicts from escalating into full-scale war. But clearly, any upgrading of their military capabilities surely will increase the likelihood of a disastrous outcome should they engage in another war fought between them. India's economic growth and influence in the international markets are dependent on peaceful and stable relationships with its neighbours along with a secure Indian Ocean. However China's close ties with Pakistan, especially the sale of the eight submarines, put India in a defensive posture and in view of its volatile relationship with Pakistan, India will have no option but to further augment its military strength and the weaponry of its naval fleet in defence of its national interests.

One final note worthy of future consideration is briefly summarised here. In the subcontinent's regional tinderbox that holds the elements of instantaneous conflict between India and Pakistan, the US has exercised a policy of seeking and destroying terrorist by the use of drones. The killing of Osama bin Laden in Pakistan was hailed by the US a victory for justice. However not all agree the use of drones can be legally justified. It is argued that violations of territorial integrity and the security of the people of Pakistan can only fan the flames of hatred and polarisation. Arguably, the bewildered people of Pakistan are driven to see China as their champion in their struggle for security and prosperity. The Chinese Premier Wen Jia Bao while visiting Pakistan in December 2010 condemned the use of drones by the US and added:

> Pakistan has made huge sacrifices and an important contribution to the international fight against terrorism, that its independence, sovereignty, and territorial integrity must be respected, and that the international community should understand and support Pakistan's efforts to maintain domestic stability and to realise its economic and social development. China is ready to assist Pakistan and its population to weather their political and economic troubles.

Map 1: India's disputed borders with China.

Note: The dashed areas in the map are the disputed borders with China's Tibet. The Aksai Chin is the dashed area in north India, and the Arunachal Pradesh is the dashed area to the right of Bhutan.

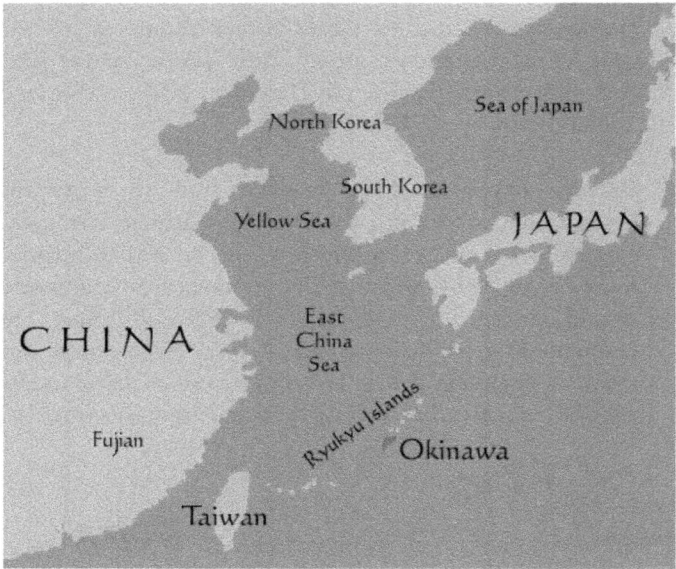

Map 2: Japan's Ryukyu Islands in the East China Sea.

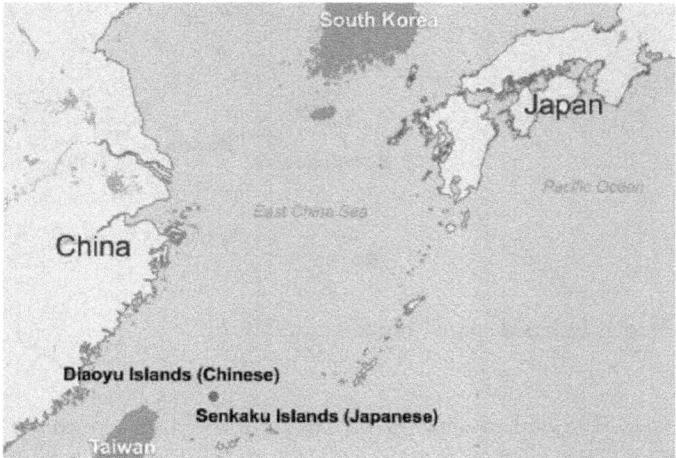

Map 3: China's claim of sovereignty over the Diaoyu Islands.

Chapter VI

Relations with the West

Let us turn our attention to China's relations with the West. There have risen vociferous voices in the West addressing the positions many Western countries have taken in their trade relations with China. The assumptions that trade with China is beneficial to the common Western citizen have come to be challenged on the basis that the trade benefits are not reflected uniformly across the social spectrum but tend to apply mostly to the select few at the top of the industrial pyramid, e.g., coal, gas and oil industry magnates.

Canada

Globally, Chinese trade with the West has generated billions of US$ surpluses that have propelled China into becoming the world's second largest economy after the United States, and the projections are that within the foreseeable future China will surpass the US into first position. The policies that China has applied to achieve such a dominant position in worldwide commerce are the simple applications of 'psychological dominance and exploitation of the enemy's weaknesses and harming enemy morale by breaking or shifting alliances.' In the first instance, the dazzled eyes of Western companies see China's 1.3 billion inhabitants a treasure trove of immense value hence enter into the quagmire of the Chinese economy with no guarantees on future terms. This gives the extant or any future Chinese government unqualified discretionary rights to withdraw trading rights of a foreign company without recourse. On such basis the government of China, through the use of its regulatory powers, provides financial incentives to foreign companies investing in China but only to the extent that the incentives made available to the investors produce enormous positive returns to China, otherwise trading rights and the associated incentives are withdrawn. But often incentives are predicated on transfer of Western technology to mainland China as a condition of doing business and, usually, under the constantly probing eyes of Chinese authorities. The fundamental weakness of any Western company exploited by China under these circumstances is the company's obsession with the prospects of enormous profits from the perceived huge Chinese market, and the fears that if it 'does not jump on the band wagon, someone else will.' A case in point is the record of Canada's two-way trading partnership with China. China continues to export hi-tech products to Canada, such as personal computers, smart phones, video recording devices, electrical machinery and mechanical appliances, to name a few. While these are often products of Western technology transfers employed in China, Canada still mainly exports agricultural produce to China - apart from ores and organic chemicals that vitally drive China's industry forward - thus causing large unprecedented deficits in Canada's trade with China. Figures published by the Asia Pacific Foundation of Canada show the alarming deficits in Canada's trade balance with China in just over a single fiscal year - from a deficit of C$ 28.6 billion in 2014 to a deficit of C$ 34.3 billion in 2015.[1]

The United States

China's relationship with the United States, on the other hand, is much complicated and also on a higher political level and may be viewed as quietly confrontational. Their annual trading balance, which is dramatically in favour of China, has grown from a mere US$ 6 million in 1985 to a phenomenal figure near US$ 340 billion in 2015.[2] For a perspective on this deficit, it should be noted that the total outstanding public debt of the United States in 2016 approached US$ 19 trillion of which US$ 1.3 trillion was owed to China.

In an effort to appreciate how China can achieve such monumental financial advantages in open Western market capitalist economy, it is important to note that the arguments discussed in the previous paragraph concerning Canada are still valid in China's *modus operandi* with the United States. Here, additionally, we must include China's use of the further tenets of *The Art of War* 'harming enemy morale by breaking or shifting alliances' and 'to subdue the enemy without fighting' which advises ways for gaining the upper hand against an adversary. How did China implement the use of these tenets?

No doubt Chinese intellectuals and their think tank counterparts were aware of Charles P. Kindleberger, George Modelski and Robert Gilpin's academic studies of Hegemonic Stability Theory which indicates that the international community and its systems are more likely to remain stable when a single nation-state is the dominant world power; thus the construct word - hegemony.[3,4] In the time period between the founding of early recorded civilisations and the late 1700s CE, it was impossible for one empire to dominate the entire globe, largely because of inability to communicate rapidly and reach effectively across large distances. The Greek and Roman empires, the Islamic caliphates and the Mongol Empire fell at least partly because their occupied land spaces were too large to allow effective control. Hegemony exists, therefore, when a single state, or a civilisation, can extend its political, economic, social and cultural influences over others, and is able to exercise its power either through diplomacy, coercion, or persuasion and can single-handedly dominate the rules and arrangements of engagements internationally. China's grand scheme began when it struck a strategic bargain in its bilateral stability relationship with the US by conceding to the US hegemony in running world affairs in return for the US not to interfere in China's economic and domestic political developments. This 'alliance' with the US guaranteed regional (Asia-Pacific) stability under the American defence umbrella but most importantly allowed China the opportunity to vigorously pursue peaceful alliances with nations that traditionally had looked towards the West for trade. In the early 20th century the United States was South-east Asia's largest trade partner, but today it is China.

China's earliest efforts for moving forward with its agendas began earnestly in November 2000 when it proposed the idea of a regional Asian free trade area - on the model established in Shenzhen by Deng Xia Ping quarter of a century earlier. Only two years later China achieved a measure of success when an initial framework agreement was signed in November 2002 in the capital of Cambodia, Phnom Penh, with the implicit intention to follow through with establishing a free trade area between China and the ASEAN (an acronym for the Association of South-east Asian Nations) that will represent an agreement amongst a total of eleven participating Asian nations. The full free trade area came into effect on 1 January 2010 and it included Brunei, Burma (Myanmar), Cambodia, Indonesia, Laos, Malaysia, Philippines, Singapore, Thailand, Vietnam and the People's Republic of China. Subsequently, Chinese investments increased dramatically in what had come to be known since the mid-1990s as the 'Bamboo Network' (a network of Chinese businesses operating in the markets of South-east Asia). One significant outcome of China-ASEAN agreement was China's nationalistic propagation of the idea that the member states were sharing common family and cultural ties.[5] The following quote accurately places the origins and the essence of China's imposing nationalism:

> This has become a timely question. After a couple of bad centuries, China is back. It believes, with some justification, that for most of its history it was the largest, wealthiest, best governed, and technologically most advanced society on the planet. China brims with confidence that it can regain this status, which it considers the natural order of affairs, and that it will do so in this century. Analogies to other rising powers with shallower histories — France, the United States, Germany, Japan, the USSR — are not helpful in predicting the consequences of China's rise. China has no messianic ideology to export; no doctrine of 'manifest destiny' to advance; no belief in social Darwinism or imperative of territorial expansion to act upon; no cult of the warrior to animate militarism or glorify war; no exclusion from contemporary global governance to overcome; no satellite states to garrison; no overseas colonies or ideological dependencies to protect; no history of power projection or military intervention beyond its immediate frontiers; no entangling alliances or bases abroad.[6]

Taking note of China's bulbous trade with its regional neighbours with a value that had expanded from US$ 60 billion in 2003 to a record US$ 193 billion in 2008, the United States soon recognised the damaging impact of China-ASEAN pact on its foreign trade welfare, and the geopolitical contest into which the US had been drawn simply by China's creation of the regional economic integration with the specific exclusion of the United States under its hegemonic agreement. The stage was set for the US to take the necessary steps to counteract the impact of the China-ASEAN pact. The urgency of action was underscored by China's willingness to project military power in the region, and by US's commitments to protect its 'Pacific Rim' allies. Thus a central foreign policy to address China's not-so-quiet challenge, that came to be known as 'Asian Pivot', became a priority. Under this policy, the US would increase its economic, military and diplomatic commitments to its much concerned allies in the East.

In principle, the appropriate action necessary to respond to China's challenge in the East was to be the creation of a set of rules and trade arrangements by the United States that would deny China participation for the foreseeable future and deliberately isolate it economically. After many years of difficult negotiations and resolving issues of conflict of interests within the relevant parties, the 'Trans Pacific Partnership' (TPP) agreement was signed on 5 October 2015. Historically, the TPP was an expansion of the 'Trans-Pacific Strategic Economic Partnership' agreement, which was signed by Brunei, Chile, New Zealand, and Singapore in 2005. But ultimately, Australia, Canada, Japan, Malaysia, Mexico, Peru, Vietnam and the United States signed the agreement bringing the total number of participating countries to twelve. The trade areas that the agreement covered included comprehensive market access, regional approach to commitments, addressing new trade challenges, platform for regional integration and inclusive trade with reduction in tariffs and the protection of intellectual property.

With regards to the last item - the protection of intellectual property - there is much evidence accusing China of taking advantage of its massive trade relation with ASEAN members who are also members of the TPP. Official reports to the United States Congress apparently have stated that there are several thousand Chinese operatives in the 'Bamboo Network' and in US companies which are engaged in covert activities for acquiring state-of-the-art Western technology applicable exclusively to military purposes. It is believed that the same situation is also true in the industries of the US's major trade partner, Canada. No doubt, China dismisses such allegations but suspicions linger and concerns remain even about the role of advanced Chinese students and visiting scientists who are admitted annually to major universities on the North American continent.

Technology espionage perpetrated by China is a major threat to Western innovation and the problem seems insolvable despite massive and extended litigations. Chinese judicial offices do not release details of case rulings until a significant time has elapsed by which time often culprits go unpunished or appeals are curtailed by the lack of clarity of the facts judicially considered that had lead to a verdict. A case in point was the NBC television's broadcast of *60 Minutes* on 17 January 2016 reporting a clear case of espionage which has caused the loss of jobs of more than 600 Americans and the near collapse of the multi-million dollar company that formerly employed them. AMSC, an American firm that makes software to run wind turbines had provided for a number of years the software that operated wind turbines manufactured by the Chinese firm Sinovel. The AMSC's upgraded version of its latest software that was still under development and not ready for release was discovered, to the dismay of AMSC, being used by Sinovel in some of the operating turbines in the field thus denying AMSC both financial compensation and patent rights. The culprit, an employee of AMSC was arrested and indicted for espionage, a case which has been validated by Western authorities. Yet the Chinese courts on the island of Hainan have denied a ruling, based on what is claimed to be insufficient evidence of theft, and instead have advised arbitration. The culprit, on the other hand, has sought refuge in China with significant improvement in the quality of his life as judged by his domestic environment complete with a new Chinese wife.

Cleary, TPP has not been entirely successful in delivering its defined objectives, nor has it allayed the fears of its South-eastern members from China's rising political power. China had lulled its neighbours for more than a decade by virtue of its ability to raise the standard of living and wealth of its neighbours while gradually broadening its claims of undisputed sovereignty especially over the South China Sea, a major transport artery of global trade. But China, as expected, describes the relation with its neighbours as one of peaceful coexistence, respectful of their sovereignty and culture. Yet, a former foreign minister of Thailand has remarked 'the picture does not look good. Over the past 10 and 20 years we were concentrating on the economic side. Suddenly over the past few years China claims that it owns the South China Sea.' The ASEAN's concern over these matters seem to be consistent as indicated by a report issued by the Institute of Security and International Studies in Bangkok that describes ASEAN relationship with China as 'talking past each other. They don't have a common starting point and there are very different interpretations of facts on the ground. It's very dangerous. There is a lot of mistrust.'

In the context of China's potential military objectives, again we return to Deng Xiao Ping and invoke his words of the 1990s that came to be known as the '24 Character Strategy.' In this he advises 'Observe calmly; secure our position; cope with affairs calmly; hide our capacities and bide our time; be good at maintaining a low profile; and never claim leadership.' It behoves us to compare Deng Xiao Ping's words with the advice given by Sun Tzu in *The Art of War*: 'Hence that general is skilful in attack whose opponent does not know what to defend; and he is skilful in defence whose opponent does not know what to attack.' The intent of this strategy, which came on the heels of the collapse of the former Soviet Union, was to instil in the Chinese polity the means of quietly protecting China's national interests while continuing its expanded interactions with the West in the absence of its formidable communist ally. To many Western democracies this has been viewed as an ominous statement of China's foreign policy strategy of long-term plans with undeclared content and purpose, covertly aimed at building up China's deterrent capability without exposing a large offensively superior visible force. Naturally, China has rejected this view and has offered alternative explanation and benign interpretation of Deng's words. Given the various aspects of China's massive interactions throughout the world along with their accompanying thought-provoking discussions, which have been the subject of the discourse herein, it is no wonder that the alternative interpretations offered by China are at best suspect. The words of the current president of China reverberate with the echoes of China's past leaders and resonate with his clarion call for the 'great rejuvenation of the Chinese civilisation.' Several facts seem to run parallel with these words. Beijing has openly publicised the state's modernisation objectives called the 'Two Centenary Goals.' The first centenary goal is to be met by 2020 CE when China hopes to have achieved for example, a 60% urbanisation rate; construction of manned Chinese space station; transition to clean energy and its first domestically-built aircraft carrier. In short, China is projected to be by 2020 a modernised 21st century internationally recognised power on par with the US. Perhaps most importantly, to achieve this objective China had intended by 2020 to have doubled its 2010 GDP figure of US$ 6 trillion. We should take notice however that for the whole of 2016 China's nominally estimated GDP is expected to exceed US$ 12 trillion, well ahead of Beijing's plan delineated for the first centenary goal. How valid are the above arguments regarding China's covert foreign policy strategy of long-term plans?

In the context of the above paragraphs, it is appropriate at this point to demonstrate to the reader what can be clearly seen as China's practice of the concept of stratagem, intent on avoiding confrontation and managing global perceptions. Although the following quotation is disclaimed by the broadsheet *China Daily*, the author Doug Bandow[7] and for the *China Daily*, Zhang Hai Jun, appear to write from a pacifist position in an effort to amass a world opinion in the affirmative to China's covert ambitions. Below is part verbatim quotation from a larger contribution:

In short, in the near to middle term, at least, in any real sense the US has little to fear from China. Even if Beijing desired to threaten the US homeland, conquer US territories or interdict US commerce, it has little ability to do so. What China seeks is to end Washington's dominance along the former's coast, *[this author: Why? and defensive against what?]* an objective more defensive than offensive.

And economics is on Beijing's side. It is far costlier to project power than to deter its use. How much is Washington willing to spend to maintain the overwhelming military superiority necessary to impose its will on China throughout the latter's own region? Such a military is going to grow less affordable over time.

The US Congressional Budget Office predicts trillion dollar annual deficits within a decade and rising outlays on entitlements in future years. Are Americans prepared to sacrifice domestic needs for defence, not of their own nation but of allied states that underfund their own militaries?

The US and China will inevitably have disagreements. However, they have no vital interest in conflict. Indeed, there is no serious cause for conflict if Washington is willing to accommodate China's rise. The US government's primary duty is to protect Americans' interests, not Washington's influence.'[†]

[†] Zhang Hai Jun is a senior fellow of the Cato Institute. The Cato Institute is an American libertarian think tank headquartered in Washington, D.C. It was founded as the Charles Koch Foundation in 1974.

Steel and Aluminium

China's old agrarian-based economy and its reliance on man-powered non-mechanised production modes that left the nation inferior to the West's Industrial Revolution are now relegated to the annals of Chinese history. Today's Chinese steel, aluminium, automotive, textile and petrochemical industries are the bedrock upon which China's economy is founded and which sustains its competitive edge in the global markets. The steel industry, in particular, is considered a measure of China's economic health; it is also a symbolic measure of China's industrial power. Today, China's steel production is almost ten times larger than the US's steel output, and as big as the rest of the world's steel industry combined.

The growth and expansion of Chinese steel production began in the 1970s when Deng Xiao Ping adopted the market-oriented economic policy for China. Its position as a major global steel producer began with the founding of the steel-maker Shanghai Bao Shan Steel which in 2009 stood as the world's second largest steel producer after Arcelor-Mittal with headquarters in Luxemburg. South Korea, Japan and India stood third, fourth and fifth, respectively.[8] In comparison, the largest of the two US steel producer in 2009, US Steel Corporation, was ranked eleventh.

In recent years the Chinese steel production has surged far beyond China's domestic needs and its negative impact on US's steel economy - and Europe's as well - resides in the dumping of the huge excess capacity into the global markets thus leading to significant trade friction. The fiscal aspects of this international friction are beyond the subject of this book. The Chinese government has indicated it would curtail the rate of its steel production to maintain some form of an international balance, but to date there have been no indications that any action has been taken. Furthermore, despite Chinese government's commitment to reduce its rate of steel production, its exports in the first five months of the current year are expected to see another record year for Chinese steel. Although a number of privately owned steel companies in the north-east of China stand abandoned and derelict, almost all of the state-owned steel producers continue to feed the export market. Their massive debts are rolled-over by the state to keep thousands of its employees from roaming jobless in the streets.

The issue of the aluminium industry in the US is not much different from that of China's steel industry. Pennsylvania's former Democratic Congressman Ronald Klink has described quite graphically the plight of the town of New Kensington which had become practically a ghost town suffering from high crime, drug abuse and the inevitable sequel, prostitution. This was a place where American jobs once flourished, where innovative aluminium products were developed for the aeronautical and automotive industries. But, in 2015 nearly 3,500 aluminium workers in New Kensington lost their jobs and many more remain under threat as a result of Chinese aluminium overcapacity and unfair subsidisation. Michael Bless, president of Century Aluminium, stated in late 2015 that 'This industry is key to the US economy and the aggressive and illegal subsidies China provides to its state-owned industry are posing a risk to tens of thousands of American jobs.' He has claimed that 50% of the American aluminium smelters remaining in operation by the end of 2015, three-quarters of them will make significant production cutbacks and associated layoffs.

In late 2015, the last remaining US aluminium smelter, producer of high purity aluminium - which is used in key components in US military hardware - announced that it was reducing production by over 60% with the loss of 400 American jobs. Is it conceivable that ending the production of high purity aluminium in the US may put America's national security interests at risk? Should the US rely on importing this critical metal from potentially adversarial countries?

Chapter VII

Dark Propositions

Africa

The Chinese bureaucratic apparatus is fundamentally managed by several government agencies under the strict dictates of the National Congress of the Communist Party of China.† The Ministry of Foreign Affairs and the Ministry of Commerce are the two agencies principally charged with managing China's African affairs. As is obvious from the agencies' titles, the former is assigned to deal with political affairs while the latter deals with economic matters. The race for China to establish a firm globally meaningful presence in Africa, both politically and commercially, has been the source of constant friction between the two agencies as they race to promote China's international image as a philanthropic and a reliable ally. Nevertheless, during the last few years there has been a substantial increase in China's investments and interest in Africa where often commercial interests have undermined

---

† The congress represents the highest authoritative body within the Communist Party of China and meets about once every five years to sanction important national decisions that define the nation's future political and domestic directions.

other Chinese national interests. In the main, the investments have served politically well for China as they have helped meet Africa's needs for funding infrastructure, housing and revenue-producing projects - an example of the latter is the construction of China's first overseas military outpost in Djibouti which will be discussed below. However, many Western economists and policy analysts have become increasingly concerned about the concentration of China's investments in African oil, mineral and other natural resources that conflict with Africa's long-term sustainable social stability and improved governance. More importantly, however, many questions have been raised regarding the true underlying objectives China may want to achieve beyond its needs for natural resources as it becomes a global economic and political power. It may be assumed that within China's overall foreign policy agendas, economic assistance to African nations may represent the core of China's geopolitical strategic positioning ambitions that will give China in the long-term an assertive voice in the international arena dealing with its security and with the longevity of its own political ideology. Moreover, China may see many of the non-democratic politically fragile African countries as fertile grounds where China can promote the 'Chinese model' of a successful one-party dictatorial state thus securing for itself potentially long-term supportive political camaraderie. Also, a strong social element that China may think contributes to reinforcing this camaraderie is the commonality of China's historical victimisation by Western colonialism with Africa's own centuries-old history of its subjugation and exploitation by Western imperialism.

Djibouti

Historically China had been mostly an insular nation concerned primarily with protecting its national borders. For centuries throughout the Chinese civilisation, China had not established colonies far from its borders, did not have an ideology which it wanted disseminated and even lacked a discernible nationalism. In the 15th century China's massive sea-going armadas sailed the Indian Ocean under the command of their famous Admiral Zheng He, who in the early 1400s led a large Chinese expeditionary fleet across the Indian Ocean and reached the waters of the Arabian Sea and the eastern shores of Africa.[1] Yet, his return to the Ming dynasty China was celebrated not for his military achievements and colonisation of Africa some 8,000 kilometres away, but for the contents of the exotic African goods laden in his ships. In the centuries that followed, China lost its seafaring supremacy and ultimately capitulated to the technologies achieved by the West as a result of the Industrial Revolution in Northern Europe.

The lack of Chinese historical ambitions for colonising far away foreign lands and its traditional focus exclusively on maintaining and defending its unified sovereign nation made a dramatic shift when in November 2015 China's President Xi Jin Ping announced China would establish its first overseas military installation in the East African nation of Djibouti, in the Horn of Africa. Although Chinese Ministry of Foreign Affairs described the installation simply as an outpost which would be used to supply Chinese naval ships patrolling the Arabian Sea on anti-piracy duty, it is not difficult to see through this smokescreen the implications of this policy predicated as a naval supply station. The great distances of the installation from mainland China make Djibouti an unlikely site for the announced intended purpose where a more practical, centrally located supply installation is available to China by treaty in south-western Pakistan. No doubt piracy has been a problem in recent years in the Gulf of Aden. But the Djibouti site is on the west side of the Gulf of Aden while the piracies have occurred across from Oman (in the Arabian Sea) and no less than 1,500 kilometres east of Djibouti. The piracy sites clearly bisect the seas between Pakistan's south-western shores and Djibouti and raise questions about the Djibouti installation's usefulness in combating piracy. Furthermore, the implied purpose of the site far away from China's command centres in Beijing deviates from China's traditional focus on protecting its immediate national borders. And, also, the establishment of this military installation is a break with China's long-standing policy of projecting itself as a peace-seeking nation not interested in emulating the United States in building military bases abroad. So, what can be deduced regarding the potentially hidden purpose(s) behind China's selection of Djibouti as a contractual military base?

The assignment of the base at Djibouti, strategically located at the extreme south end of the Red Sea, may have been a prelude to the anticipated alliances China was preparing to pursue in the Middle East once the expected lifting of the sanctions on Iran had come into effect. Indeed the multiple business and industrial cooperative agreements signed by President Xi in the Middle East during his recent state visits to Saudi Arabia, Egypt and Iran are indications of China's recognition of the importance of the Middle East and that neglecting it could derail China's strategic march towards becoming a global superpower. It is not unreasonable to suggest that Xi's apparent interest in diffusing the time-bomb of the recent conflict between Saudi Arabia and Iran is China's public pronouncement of equal friendship with their large, rigid and staunch Muslim populations of Shi'a and Sun'ni sects. Similar overtures and innuendos made by China in helping resolve the conflict in Afghanistan, and possibly involving Pakistan, fit the same general perception China may wish to project. There might be multiple reasons why China may wish to promote this perception, but two stand out from the crowd. The first, and potentially the most important, is Xi's proposal in October 2013 of resurrecting the economic ties that existed along the ancient 'Silk Road' which he termed 'One Belt, One Road.' This historically was a series of connected mercantile ventures that linked Xi'an in Shaanxi province, through Islamic Central Asia to the Middle East via Tehran (Iran) and Damascus (Syria) and then on to Constantinople (today's Istanbul, Turkey), the gateway to Rome and the wider European markets. In September 2015 the title of Xi's proposal was fixed as 'Belt and Road' and was described as an initiative rather than a strategy.

Further aspects of Xi's proposal will be presented below. Keeping in mind that the vast majority of the population in Xinjiang province is composed of ethnic Muslim Uyghur of Central Asian origin, the second reason perhaps is that it seems prudent on the part of China to improve its image and friendship with the countries of Central Asia in order to pacify the restless Muslims in Xinjiang who have in recent years aspired for independence from China by way of social unrest, killings and confrontations with the majority Han authorities in the province.

To some, the Djibouti base poses in the long run a potential threat to US interests and capabilities in the Middle East. US Army General David Rodriguez, who is a commander with U.S. Africa Command, argues that China has long had an economic foothold in Africa, but the base at Djibouti would be an expansion of its military prowess beyond the Asia-Pacific region. He further believes the Chinese base would be a logistics hub; it would allow China to improve its ability to gather intelligence in the region and beyond, such as parts of the Middle East, the Arabian Peninsula and Central Africa. According to J. Peter Pham, director of the Africa Centre at the Atlantic Council, not only would China save money by building its own military base in Djibouti, it would also increase its global stature. An alternate opinion is expressed by Senator Chris Coons, Democrat, State of Delaware, a senior member of the Senate Foreign Relations Subcommittee on African Affairs, who believes 'Overall, China's presence in Africa is certainly something we need to pay more attention to -- but not just in Djibouti. Africa's middle class is growing faster than ever and the continent offers great opportunities for partnerships between both governments and the private sector. We don't want to lose out on those opportunities to Chinese companies or the Chinese government.' But this recommendation should be assessed in light of China's level of economic interest in Africa. True, China-Africa bilateral trade in 2000 was around US$ 10 billion and by 2014 it had exploded to more than US$ 200 billion. But in reality, Africa thus far represents a tiny 3% and 5% of China's global investment and trade respectively.

Regarding Djibouti, we must consider one final observation which is open not only to kaleidoscopic interpretations but must also be viewed with great circumspect. The intriguing observation is that Djibouti also hosts a small US military base at Camp Lemonnier. It is the only permanent US military base in Africa acquired from the French military in 2001 soon after the World Trade Centre crisis in New York City in September of that year. Ironically, the US navy defines the purpose of the camp as a support facility for preparing naval ships and aircraft, and for regional and combatant command requirements. How did China fit into this picture in 2015?

Belt and Road Initiative

The 'Belt and Road' initiative is based on an economic analogy to the ancient 'Silk Road' that transported Chinese goods by camel caravans traversing across China's neighbouring Central Asian countries. It is conceived to develop a 21st century land-bound economic network connecting China to Europe primarily through the economic intermediary of China's Central Asian neighbouring countries leading initially to the markets of the Middle East and North Africa. This initiative would supplement China's current fragile and politically volatile maritime trade routes but more importantly it will provide China a level of security by drawing its neighbours into its sphere of political influence, and also by preventing intrusion into these areas by politically hostile forces.

The ancient trade routes known as the Silk Road, linked the opposite ends of the known world during the second half of the first Christian millennium – the empire of China in the east and Europe in the west. As is true for most modes of transport, there were branch routes from the main thoroughfares of the Silk Road which led to important destinations, such as India in the south and Tashkent and Samarqand in the north. But, it should be borne in mind that numerous trading posts, oasis towns and open markets scattered all across Central Asia linked countless countries and communities with China. These staging links, like the sequentially connected beads of a Buddhist prayer ring, were lined up along the trading routes of the Silk Road and formed the strategic facilities that permitted goods to be exchanged in relative safety throughout the known world

The development of the Silk Road and its ultimate demise occurred in two stages. Although the origins of the Silk Road can be traced to the 2nd century BCE, the first significant stage of its growth began in the 2nd century CE and reached its zenith in the 6th century CE. During this period the dynamics of the trade along the roads encouraged a wider regional participation that eventually created two major alternate routes, one called the Southern Branch of the Silk Road, and the other the Northern Branch. Very few merchants would venture to travel the full length of the perilous and complex roads stretching over a distance exceeding 8,000 kilometres across deserts and high-mountain passes. Ordinarily, the journey would take more than a year for the few who dared to tread the road from Xi'an to Damascus. The majority of the traders however were local residents of settlements through which the trade routes meandered their way west. They would travel from their home markets to one in an adjacent market where they would exchange their goods and then return home within a few days of absence.

The second stage era was essentially defined by the vast and lucrative trading activities that continued to thrive and then gradually decline through the Tang dynasty period. Subsequently, the decline in the use of the Silk Road continued and was accelerated by the opening of the sea routes. The ultimate demise of the Silk Road's utility came with the regional devastations brought about by the early conquests of the Mongol hordes spearheaded by Genghis Khan. What remained standing of the abandoned oasis towns laid to waste, was eventually engulfed by the endlessly shifting sands of the surrounding deserts.

The term Silk Road, in German '*Seidenstrasse*,' was coined in 1877 by the German explorer and geographer Baron Ferdinand von Richthofen to describe the ancient trade routes across sandy emporia nestled in the deserts of China and in the foot-hills of snow-capped mountains in Central Asia. Although silk was a major commodity that was exchanged with the West, the trade in fact was much more diversified in content. Hence the term Silk Road is, in a manner, a misnomer. During the Middle Ages the wealthy Pisan, Venetian and Genoese city-states monopolised the bulk of the Mediterranean trading networks by striking alliances with many regional powers that gave the city-states exclusive trading rights that linked their interests with the pivotal Near Eastern triad cities of Constantinople, Alexandria and Damascus. The exports from China included silk, silken fabric, herbs, spices, lacquer, porcelain, painted stoneware and bronze. In exchange China imported glass from Europe, ivory from Africa, precious stones and mineral dyes from India and lapis lazuli from Afghanistan.

A quick appreciation of the calculated value of the 'Belt and Road' initiative would have on the current and future Chinese world economic control can be gained by identifying the actual historic geographic sites that supported the mercantile activities along the ancient Silk Road. First, the trading activities began in the historic capital of Xi'an in Shaanxi province and headed west to the city of Lanzhou in Gansu province then continued across the province's western oasis posts of Wuwei, Zhangye, Yumen, respectively, and finally Anxi in the extreme north-west of the province not far from the eastern border of Xinjiang province. There the road was divided into a Southern branch and a Northern branch. From Anxi the road proceeded south-westerly through the Buddhist community in Dunhuang then crossed into Miran in Xinjiang province. From Miran the road turned directly west and progressed along the Southern Branch of the road running between the southern edge of the Taklamakan Desert and the northern slopes of Altun and Kunlun mountains. It then passed through the Xinjiang province oasis towns of Chakilik, Cherchen, Niya, Khotan, Yarkand and finally reached Kashgar in Xinjiang province's frontiers with the Pamir Mountains not far from the borders of Kazakhstan, Kyrgyzstan, Tajikistan, Afghanistan and Pakistan. Alternatively, the trading caravans left Dunhuang and began to use sometime in the 4th century the less perilous Northern Branch along the luscious foothills of the Tian Shan Mountains. Their first oasis was Hami followed by Turpan, Korla, Kuqa, Aksu, respectively, all in Xinjiang province, and finally joined the Southern Branch in Kashgar.

Kashgar was a staging town for the caravans for their trek across Central Asia. This was made possible by three high-mountain passes; north-westerly was Torugart Pass in the Tian Shan Mountains that gave access to the Uzbek cities of Tashkent, Samarqand and Bukhara; westerly was Erkashtam Pass in the Pamir Mountains that gave access to the cities of Balkh in northern Afghanistan and Merv in Turkmenistan; and Khunjerap Pass in the Karakorum mountain range that gave access to Taxila in the district of Punjab in Pakistan. Across the Hindu Kush Mountains from Taxila the caravans reached India in the south and Kabul, Afghanistan in the north.

In view of the above descriptions of the interactive trading regions of ancient times which were made possible by the Silk Road, it should at once become clear the political and commercial significance of the 'Belt and Road' initiative which the Chinese Communist Party's Central Committee had approved on 12 November 2013 as follows:

> We will set up development-oriented financial institutions; accelerate the construction of infrastructure connecting China with neighbouring countries and regions, and work hard to build a Silk Road Economic Belt and a Maritime Silk Road.

Initiative or a Strategy?

The 'Belt and Road' initiative would encompass the modern countries of Kazakhstan, Kyrgyzstan, Tajikistan, Uzbekistan, Turkmenistan, Afghanistan, Pakistan and possibly Russia. Note the layout of the Belt and Road initiative, in comparison to the routes taken by the ancient Silk Road, which in fact seemed designed for the belt routes to go through all the above countries and ultimately reach Europe. Thus, the initiative is proposed to proceed from China in three directions via northern, central and southern paths. The northern path will go through Central Asia then in a north-western direction through Russia reach Europe. The central belt will go through Central Asia then in a south-western direction through Iran and the Persian Gulf reach the Mediterranean. The southern path will proceed towards the south-east to South Asia and the Indian Ocean. Naturally, China's trade agreements along the belt countries in the context of linked trade facilities, free trade zones, tariff arrangements, financial integration and currency regulations, import-export types and limits and increased diplomatic coordination would give China a massive advantage in seeing its exports reach the four corners of the world while importing what China would need to propel its march to world supremacy under the guise of shared interests and prosperity. So, if the Belt and Road initiative becomes successful, keeping in mind that it is perceived as a long-term objective, it would make China a major diplomatic force by bringing Central Asia and Eastern Europe into a cohesive union and by integrating their resultant immense economic strength with China's own. Such an outcome in the globalised world markets can potentially cast an intriguing political shadow over all European interests in Central Asia, the Near East and the Mediterranean Basin.

The embassy of the People's Republic of China in the Republic of Azerbaijan released on 3 March 2015 the following communiqué issued jointly by China's National Development and Reform Commission, Ministry of Foreign Affairs, and Ministry of Commerce:

> The initiative to jointly build the Belt and Road, embracing the trend towards a multi-polar world, economic globalization, cultural diversity and greater IT application, is designed to uphold the global free trade regime and the open world economy in the spirit of open regional cooperation. It is aimed at promoting orderly and free flow of economic factors, highly efficient allocation of resources and deep integration of markets; encouraging the countries along the Belt and Road to achieve economic policy coordination and carry out broader and more in-depth regional cooperation of higher standards; and jointly creating an open, inclusive and balanced regional economic cooperation architecture that benefits all. Jointly building the Belt and Road is in the interests of the world community. Reflecting the common ideals and pursuit of human societies, it is a positive endeavour to seek new models of international cooperation and global governance, and will inject new positive energy into world peace and development.

> The Belt and Road Initiative aims to promote the connectivity of Asian, European and African continents and

their adjacent seas, establish and strengthen partnerships among the countries along the Belt and Road, set up all-dimensional, multi-tiered and composite connectivity networks, and realize diversified, independent, balanced and sustainable development in these countries. The connectivity projects of the Initiative will help align and coordinate the development strategies of the countries along the Belt and Road, tap market potential in this region, promote investment and consumption, create demands and job opportunities, enhance people-to-people and cultural exchanges, and mutual learning among the peoples of the relevant countries, and enable them to understand, trust and respect each other and live in harmony, peace and prosperity.

Is the Belt and Road initiative a step towards creating a China-led regional coalition which might be perceived as a defensive land-mass security buffer zone surrounding China's vulnerable western and southern frontiers? On the other hand, many foreign observers of China's rise view the Belt and Road as a cloaked strategy to extend China's geopolitical influence. One could imagine China's initial plans to achieve this influence would naturally begin with involving its closest neighbours through their integration into a system of economic and political framework whose ripple-effect would in time enlarge and extend the integration of countries further a field. However, China sees the Belt and Road idea as a mechanism for integrating the people and cultures of Central Asia and Eastern Europe into a harmonious coexistence rather than despairingly dividing their loyalties, as well as a means to focus their attentions on common economic growth rather than as political contenders. Hence, the common objective as described by Beijing is to improve the livelihood of the citizens of the linked countries, and to promote in the current globalised world the spirit of 'win-win cooperation' amongst all participants. The proclamation of a prominent Chinese analyst is that 'China should have full confidence to proclaim to the world that the Belt and Road is a Chinese grand strategy. It is a public strategy, not a conspiratorial one.'

It is clear that in accordance with the announced intents of the Belt and Road, Beijing is able to explicitly refuse to call the initiative a strategy. By definition, an initiative is a unilateral plan initiated by an individual, an organised body of individuals or a country, to pursue a certain action, generally for a beneficial outcome, but for it to be successful will require the voluntary participation by other independent bodies that would also benefit from the initiative. Although an initiative is put in motion unilaterally, it nevertheless is at least a bilateral, if not multilateral, process. The success of an initiative is often fragile as it relies on the total commitment of the voluntary participants who otherwise may choose to terminate their participation. Hence, it seems logical why Beijing would insist on the terminology of the Belt and Road as an initiative, and in the event its objectives are clandestine, then presenting it globally in a low profile format will likely prevent unwelcome repercussions should the plan become unsuccessful.

In contrast, a strategy is a carefully laid, amply funded and politically approved plan put in place deliberately to achieve a specific goal usually, but not necessarily, with intent to achieve supremacy in a field other than for public good. It is safe to assume that common usage of strategy is synonymous with military planning coupled to a geopolitical ambition. Also, a strategy as opposed to an initiative can be exclusively a unilateral plan, but bilateral or multilateral plans are also possible. Again, these generally occur in militaristic contexts, such as in defensive alliances and in national security settings.

It is possible to assume the Belt and Road initiative may not immediately appear as a strategy designed to counter United State's recently invigorated physical involvement in South-eastern Asian political affairs. However, a slight glimpse into

China's most recent aggressive action in the South China Sea strikes smack into the very heart of China's long-term based manoeuvres with the potential to retaliate effectively and possibly pre-emptively, against any regional attempt at curtailing its rise to world dominance. The point here is China's deployment in mid-February 2016 of surface-to-air missiles on the disputed Woody Island, the largest in the Paracel Islands south-east of China's Hainan Island in the South China Sea. Sovereignty over the island is claimed by China, Taiwan and Vietnam but Beijing has emphatically insisted while categorically and unilaterally dismissing all other claims that China had a right to build self-defence systems in the strategic region claimed as part of its territorial waters of the South China Sea. Neil Ashdown, deputy editor of the global security journal *Jane's Intelligence Review*, has said his analysis of satellite imagery indicates China has deployed a fourth-generation surface-to-air system, and he has called it 'a significant military escalation.' Is this action a message to the United States and its regional allies vying for political and military position in the region? Can the world community accept China's militarisation of the South China Sea as a proper behaviour for a nation intent to 'enhance people-to-people and cultural exchanges, and mutual learning among the peoples of the relevant countries, and enable them to understand, trust and respect each other and live in harmony, peace and prosperity?' It is safe to state, therefore, that regardless of how reassuring the Chinese official rhetoric sounds, it is inevitable that many Western analysts view the Belt and Road as a geopolitical strategy with military implications. Their mantra is very clear; a nation can certainly have geopolitical interests without economic interests (United States' interests in the Philippines, Guam, Midway, Christmas Islands, etc.) but economic interests are necessarily – inevitably - geopolitical interests.

The issue of China's sovereignty over the South China Sea has placed American and Chinese naval forces virtually on continuous state of alert each jockeying for military dominance of the Pacific waters. The declared American goal is to keep the South China Sea open to all maritime traffic in the face of Beijing's claim of sovereignty over most of the 850-kilometre stretch of the sea out from the shores of mainland China. In this regard, James R. Clapper, President Obama's director of national intelligence, told the Senate Armed Services Committee in February 2016 that 'by early next year China would have a significant capacity to quickly project substantial military power to the region.' That means that shipping countries would eventually need Beijing's permission to cross the heavily trafficked South China Sea.

Origin of the Dispute

The origin of the South China Sea dispute is traced back to 1947 when the Nationalists' navy of the then Republic of China under the leadership of Chiang Kai-shek took control of many islands in the South China Sea, including Formosa (present-day Taiwan), that had been occupied by Japan prior to its defeat in the Second World War. The ensuing Chinese civil war between the Nationalists (Komintang) and the Communist (Kuntontang) ended when the Nationalists and their leader Chiang Kai-shek took refuge in the Island of Formosa on 10 December 1949, a mere seventy days after Mao Tse Tung's Communist Party had declared the founding of the People's Republic of China on 1 October 1949. Thus the newly installed Communist government in effect inherited all the nation's maritime claims in the region previously proclaimed by the Nationalists.

The gist of this dispute is what is known as the nine-dash line, an imaginary line that encircles the South China Sea which was first described by Chiang Kai-shek's Nationalist government on 1 December 1947.[2] The complete line, represented on maps as nine-dashes, comes within a few hundred kilometres of the territorial waters of Vietnam, Malaysia and Indonesia and continues to run north along the western edges of the Philippine Islands and ends at the southern tip of Taiwan. China maintains that the republic had accepted the Japanese surrender at the end of World War II and had legally reclaimed the region with the consent of the Allies, or at least, without the expressed objections of the United States and other regional claimants long before the 1982 UNCLOS treaty to which China became a signatory.[3] Moreover, China claims its fishermen were fishing in these reclaimed waters since ancient times with records of specially productive location information passed down from generation to generation. It is to be noted that when China reinforced its hold on the northern part of the region after it expelled the South Vietnamese navy from the Paracel Islands in the 1970s there was no significant reaction from the West to these events. This lack of reaction may simply be ascribed to the insularity of the People's Republic at that time hence it was not perceived as a potential economic or military threat to the new world order. Ironically, perhaps intentionally, Beijing has never defined its explicit rights within the nine-dash line region apart from China's claim of sovereignty thus leaving a measure of ambiguity. It is likely that because of this ambiguity, China has insisted on its offer of open negotiations with its neighbouring claimants, without the intrusion of a third party, with the view to reach an amicable diplomatic solution acceptable to all.

The Encounter at Sea

No doubt we, and certainly the world at large, are uneasily concerned about what would take place in an event whereby China sees its singularly claimed authority on the South China Sea's territorial waters has been violated. Here is an actual incident reported by Helene Cooper[4] aboard the US Navy cruiser USS *Chancellorsville* in the disputed waters off the Spratly Islands in the South China Sea:

When a Chinese frigate appeared on the horizon, bearing down on the US cruiser *Chancellorsville* from the direction of Mischief Reef, the cruiser's sailors went on full alert and took up their assigned positions throughout the ship. The situation took a more heightened status when a Chinese helicopter took off from the frigate and headed straight for the cruiser. 'This is US Navy warship on guard,' the communication ensign on board said into his radio from the ship's bridge. 'Come up on Frequency 121.5 or 243.' Ominously, the pilot refused to answer but kept circling the cruiser and eventually returned to the frigate which was still sailing towards the US cruiser. The captain of the cruiser then turned to one of his ensigns, of Chinese American extraction, and wondered in an enquiring voice about the Chinese helicopter's refusal to answer to the radio call. Eventually when the frigate was only 10 kilometres from the cruiser, the voice on the radio said 'US Navy Warship 62…This is Chinese Warship 575.' The cruiser replied 'This is US Warship 62. Good morning, sir. It is a pleasant day at sea. Over.' No response. The cruiser repeated 'This is US Warship 62. Good morning, sir. It is a pleasant day at sea. Over.' Still there was no response. The captain then turned to his Chinese American ensign and said 'You're up; they can't pretend they don't speak Chinese.' The ensign radioed in Chinese 'Chinese Warship 575, this is US Warship 62. Today is a sunny day for a sea voyage. Over.' After several minutes of silence the reply on the radio in Chinese said 'US Warship 62, this is Chinese Warship 575. Today's weather is great. It is a pleasure to meet you at sea.' The American ensign then followed also in Chinese 'This is US Warship 62. The weather is indeed great. It is a pleasure to meet you, too. Over.' However, the Chinese tone soon changed, and in English the question came 'How long have you been since departing from your home port? Over.' The cruiser replied 'Chinese Warship 575, this is US Navy Warship 62. We do not talk about our schedules. But we are enjoying our time at sea. Over.' Testing whether the Chinese frigate was openly following, the US cruiser made a turn and waited. It was not long when a junior officer aboard the cruiser shouted 'He just turned, sir.' And soon came another question from the frigate 'US Navy Warship 62, this is Chinese Navy Warship 575. Do you continue to have long-term voyage at sea? Over.' The answer to that question would have implied an inherent acknowledgement that the Chinese had the right to know. Instead the cruiser radioed 'This is US Navy Warship 62. All of our voyages are short because we enjoy our time at sea no matter how long we are away from home. Over.' The unexpected message that came on the radio next from the Chinese frigate said 'US Navy Warship 62, this is Chinese Navy Warship 575. Copy that I will be staying along with you for the following days. Over.' But the next day the Chinese frigate was replaced by a destroyer which followed the US cruiser until midnight when the *Chancellorsville* sailed away from the waters of the South China Sea.

Yet, unfortunately, the incident described above is not the only documented incident of China's conflicts in the South China Sea. An incident, reported by Joe Cochrane,[5] described that an Indonesian authority personnel from the Indonesian Ministry of Maritime Affairs and Fisheries had boarded a Chinese fishing boat named *Kway Fey*, detained the captain and eight-member crew for illegally fishing in Indonesian territorial waters without permission and were towing the seized boat to a base. At midnight on Saturday 19 March 2016 a Chinese Coast Guard vessel appeared and deliberately rammed the fishing boat in open sea in an area south-west of the Spratly Islands near the Natuna Islands north-west of Borneo. The action was an attempt to free the fishing boat from the Indonesian vessel and it succeeded in prying the fishing boat free and then sailing away leaving the arrested crew in the hands of the Indonesian authorities. This alarmingly aggressive behaviour demonstrated by the Chinese Coast Guard was not ignored by the Indonesian foreign minister who appropriately filed an official letter of protest with the Chinese Embassy in Jakarta. But as expected, the

Chinese Foreign Ministry described the area where the incident had occurred as 'traditional Chinese fishing grounds' and that its Coast Guard vessel 'had not entered Indonesian territorial waters.' Furthermore, China requested the immediate release of the detained Chinese crew and to ensure their physical safety.

The solution to such maritime incidents, while China insists it has sovereignty on a wide swathe of the South China Sea, is not a simple matter of diplomacy. Indonesia, as many other South-east Asian nations surrounding the South China Sea (Vietnam, the Philippines, Laos, Cambodia, Malaysia, etc.) has China as its largest trading partner and a major importer of its products. The economic power that China is wielding in South-east Asia and the arrogance China is demonstrating in pursuing its regional monopoly based on that power has been a source of serious dilemmas and frustrations for the ASEAN block. Although their social prosperity and economic viability depend on getting along with China, it is the unknown future that they fear most under a dominant all-powerful China. In the meantime, China continues to precipitate naval stand-offs, stand accused of fishing illegally, pursue off-shore land reclamation projects and invest military personnel and materiel in disputed areas.

Chapter VIII

Soft Power

Asian Infrastructure Investment Bank

Why is China creating a new development bank called Asian Infrastructure Investment Bank (AIIB)? The first news reports about the AIIB appeared in October 2013. Within the next twenty-four months, the Articles of Agreement - the charter which forms the legal basis for the Bank - was entered into force on 25 December 2015 and on 16 January 2016, the board of governors at their inaugural meeting in Beijing declared the bank open. Although the bank's sole aim was declared to be to support the building of infrastructure in the Asia-Pacific region, the United States has lobbied its allies not to join the AIIB. To date, the United States, Canada, Japan, South Korea and Taiwan remain outside the bank's membership. Although North Korea had submitted a request for membership, China had rejected that request. Table III lists the 57 current signatory member-states of the AIIB and those who are considered founding member-states as each has ratified the Articles of Agreement.

The arguments presented by China for taking this initiative in creating the AIIB are that Asia will have a massive infrastructure funding gap estimated by the Asia Development Bank (ADB) to approach US$ 8 trillion by the year 2020 and also state that the Asia Development Bank and the World Bank (WB) loans in the main support non-infrastructure projects, while the AIIB will focus its support exclusively on Asian infrastructure developments. Hence the ADB and the WB have extended a cautious welcome to the China-led AIIB as they see possibilities for mutual cooperation.

Based on China's massive international economic strength, no doubt, and justly, it wants greater input in and an alternative to its dealings with other globally established financial institutions most importantly with the International Monetary Fund (IMF) which China claims is dominated by American, European and Japanese interests. Reforms to give China a little more say at the IMF have been delayed for years, and even if they do go through America will still retain a dominating power. Furthermore, although China is the biggest economy in Asia, the ADB is dominated by Japan and the bank's president has always been a Japanese national. So what can be speculated about China's intentions behind promoting the massive AIIB undertaking?

Understandably, a plethora of diplomatic lobbying was quietly launched by the United States in an effort to dissuade its allies from joining the AIIB. No doubt the concern by the US was the potential challenges that the US dollar may face in the future as the world's reserve currency. The concern was also that China will use the new bank to expand its influence at the expense of America and Japan, and will potentially erode the global authority of the IMF, of the Asian Development Bank and the World Bank. Moreover, the establishment of the AIIB would detract from the Trans-Pacific Partnership that Washington had been promoting in a bid to cut through many trade barriers with the ASEAN members. The US's position was carefully crafted and disguised along the lines of operational standards and safeguards rather than the true underlying apprehensiveness of the US. It was stated as follows:

Our position on the AIIB remains clear and consistent. The United States and many major global economies all agree there is a pressing need to enhance infrastructure investment around the world. We believe any new multilateral institution should incorporate the high standards of the World Bank and the regional development banks. Based on many discussions, we have concerns about whether the AIIB will meet these high standards, particularly related to governance, and environmental and social safeguards. The international community has a stake in seeing the AIIB complement the existing architecture, and to work effectively alongside the World Bank and Asian Development Bank.

The prejudicial implications of US's objections to the founding of the AIIB were soon addressed by China's Premier Li Ke Qiang on 16 January 2016 at the inaugural meeting of the Board of Governors of the bank under the presidency of Jin Li Qun:

It is important for the AIIB to follow the trend of economic globalization and regional integration and meet needs of developing members for industrialisation and urbanisation. Staying committed to business first, government support and solid market principles, the AIIB is in a position to provide developing members with low-cost, technology-intensive, energy-efficient and environment-friendly solutions, equipment and financing support to facilitate industrialization and urbanization.

The AIIB's operational guidelines reassured by Li Ke Qiang in the above quote were nonetheless dismissed by the United States. It is interesting to note however that the leadership of the hegemonic US in world diplomacy, generally in conjunction with its closest allies, turned out to be ineffective in stemming the tide of eager nations, including the United Kingdom and Australia, willing to join the AIIB. These closest allies did in fact join the AIIB and methodically supported the establishment of the bank to the dismay and embarrassment of the US. Think tanks such as Chatham House in London and the China Studies Centre at the University of Sydney had concluded that the establishment of the China-based AIIB 'need not trigger vain geopolitical rivalries. China and the West can work successfully together to build a more prosperous, equitable economic order across the Asia-Pacific region and that the decision by the United Kingdom to join the China-instigated Asian Infrastructure Investment Bank shows overdue strategic clarity and awareness among the political establishment that foreign policy towards China should aim to advance the national interest rather than placate Britain's other allies.' Such conclusions and decisions openly expressed by the US's closest allies are simply interpreted to mean that the US can no longer dominate every political or economic direction that the world at large may choose to follow. The US can be more resilient and buoyant should it decide to work in harmony with the rising power of China. The United Kingdom and most other smaller powers had decided to join the AIIB simply because it was a matter of survival.[1] Should they not engage with China for their own financial and economic interests, it is likely that their international political stature will progressively disintegrate. In effect, it was not a matter of choice but of necessity that they have joined. But, sadly, these perspectives have been described by some as 'signalling nothing less than the end of the American century and the arrival of the Asian century.'

TABLE III: AIIB's Prospective Founding Member States†

Australia, Austria, Azerbaijan, Bangladesh, Brazil, Brunei, Cambodia, China, Denmark, Egypt, Finland, France, Georgia, Germany, Iceland, India, Indonesia, Iran, Israel, Italy, Jordan, Kazakhstan, South Korea, Kuwait, Kyrgyzstan, Laos, Luxembourg, Malaysia,* Maldives, Malta, Mongolia, Myanmar, Nepal, Netherlands, New Zealand, Norway, Oman, Pakistan, Philippines,* Poland,* Portugal, Qatar, Russia, Saudi Arabia, Singapore, South Africa,* Spain, Sri Lanka, Sweden, Switzerland, Tajikistan, Thailand,* Turkey, United Arab Emirates, United Kingdom (Great Britain), Uzbekistan and Vietnam.

The Case of a 'Special Relationship'

It is apparent that the Asian Infrastructure Investment Bank has been vastly successful in drawing many nations, such as the least expected Great Britain, closer into China's sphere of economic influence. This singularly distinctive unthinkable British action utterly astonished those who had considered Britain the closest ally of the United States ever since World War II. But in reviewing the history of these two nations, we are compelled to reach the conclusion that what is called 'a special relationship' between Britain and the US has not always been so. No doubt the US fought and earned its independence by defeating its nemesis the British Empire in their final battle on 19 October 1781 at Yorktown, New York. But a more recent history will demonstrate that between World Wars I and II the competition between these two nations for supremacy was severe. A decade after the end of World War I (in the 1930s) the imperial power of Great Britain was gasping for its last breath. The beginning of World War II in 1939 essentially

† Total number of prospective member states on 29 June 2015 was 57 of which the regional prospective member states were 37 and the non-regional prospective member states were 20. All prospective member states were signatories to the Articles of Agreement of the AIIB. Prerequisite for full membership requires ratification of the Articles of Agreement of the AIIB. Asterisks represent prospective member states which have not ratified the Articles of Agreement of the AIIB

bankrupted Britain and put an end to its role as an imperial power. Furthermore, the United States became an obstacle in denying Britain the many opportunities that arose for it during its battles in Asia to succeed in restoring the British Empire. It then became a matter of choice for Britain either to fight an unequal battle with the might of the newly acquired US military supremacy, or seek its alliance. Britain chose the latter despite its recognition that it must play a subservient role to US's hegemony. Apart from US's displeasure over Britain's rash intervention in the Suez crisis in Egypt in 1956, and the more recent British Parliament's refusal in August 2013 to join the US in any military action against Bashar al-Assad's Syria, the alliance between Britain and the US on the world political landscape has remained firm and bonded for the past seven decades. It is the strength of this alliance that challenges us to understand the reasons behind Great Britain's decision to join the AIIB in the face of US's hostility and opposition towards the founding of AIIB. Furthermore, adding insult to injury, the British decision encouraged other allies of the US - Europe, Israel, Australia, New Zealand, Turkey, etc. - to ignore the US's objection and decided to join the AIIB membership.

Britain seemingly understood the significance of China's economic rise and how participation in that economy would contribute to Britain's national interest. Its sagging service-based economic performances in the absence of its former manufacturing prowess had left Britain strapped for capital thus it could not ignore the prospect of Chinese investments in Britain to revitalise its infrastructure and create new blue-collar job opportunities for its people. Britain could see a plethora of opportunities for developing its independent economy by engaging with China rather than relying on the impotent and stagnate economy of its long-standing ally, the US. So, has Britain's vision been realised?

In 2010, the then British Prime Minister, David Cameron, during his visit of China negotiated the infusion of the first of many Chinese investments into the British economy. Rolls-Royce, the prime British manufacturer of jet engines signed a deal with China Eastern Airlines worth nearly US$ 11 million. This was followed by a varied series of Chinese investments that have ranged from a US$ 150 million investment by SinoFortone Group in the construction of a theme park in north Kent, which is expected to generate 27,000 jobs, to the US$ 25 billion investment by China General Nuclear Power Corporation in the construction of the Hinkley Nuclear Plant at Hinkley Point, Somerset, which will provide 5,600 jobs to mostly British workers. But above all the economic opportunities created by the Chinese investments in Britain, the sole and the most important benefit to Britain has been the agreement the Bank of England entered into with the People's Bank of China to undertake the foreign exchange of the Chinese renminbi - the Yuan - the equivalent of US$ 50 billion over three years through London's financial markets. This facility in the markets has defined the City of London the Western world's major hub for trading in the Chinese currency thus rivalling the City of New York. We may agree that China and Britain are global powers each with its own global vision, but it is inescapable to conclude that the British policies for engaging privately with China is a testament to how China's rise has fractured old alliances for the sake of national interests.

AIIB or TPP

Despite US's unsuccessful coercing attempts at weakening the AIIB's appeal as discussed above, the US has, in addition, used its hegemonic role to suggest that it [the US] is the world's main force for peace and stability and thus the rise of China is inherently ominous. The implied message, as a mainstream

Western perspective, is that China and its economic posturing with many Asian allies is an existential threat to the global supremacy of the West hence needs to be contained either by cooperation or confrontation.

Now, let us return to the question posed earlier; what can be speculated about China's intentions behind promoting the massive AIIB undertaking? The answer to this question can be pursued in three directions; one political, another commercial, and a third possibly in military terms. The political ramification of the AIIB is best described as an attempt by China to undermine and weaken the pacific alliances the US enjoys in South-east Asia. The best example is the alliance with South Korea. China, by far is South Korea's biggest trading partner yet South Korea is a pivotal ally on the Korean peninsula in a triad with Japan and the US. Now the question is what would a decision by South Korea to join the bank do to its relations with the US? Would membership in the AIIB undermine the tempestuous South Korea-US free trade agreement or even the South Korea-US alliance? South Korea has argued that joining the bank is not necessarily an indication of a pro-China stance but only following a pattern of self-interest decisions taken by so many other countries including the United Kingdom and Australia.

On the commercial front, the US has made long standing efforts to get South Korea to join the US-led Trans-Pacific Partnership but so far South Korea seems hesitant. Ironically though, the US stands to benefit from South Korea's intention to join the AIIB announced in March 2015. The Japanese government officials have reacted calmly to South Korea's decision to join the Chinese-led Asian Infrastructure Investment Bank and have stated that South Korea's decision was not unexpected considering their attempt to gain economic advantages ahead of Japan's possible participation. An extension of this scenario is South Korea's careful consideration of joining the US-led TPP to circumvent early US market gains by Japan.

The potential implications that the AIIB might have in military terms might be limited to weakening South Korea's pivotal alliance on the Korean peninsula in a triad with Japan and the US. By expanding South Korea's commercial and financial links with China, it is reasonable to assume that South Korea will be less inclined to posture itself as a military partner with the US whose foreign policies no doubt include restraining China's military options. Furthermore, with North Korea increasingly becoming reliant on China's material and political support, it is less likely that it will venture into a military conflict with the South. The US, however, has expressed interest in installing missile batteries in South Korea under a plan the Pentagon calls Terminal High-Altitude Area Defence (THAAD) which will be capable of destroying launched ballistic missiles, satellites and other objects in orbit. The purpose of this plan is to deny an enemy - perhaps China or North Korea - its capability for surveillance, offensive military actions or for initiating aggressive actions from space. South Korea had not been seen to be inclined to accept this plan and this decision, naturally, has not pleased the Pentagon. Again, in the long run, South Korea might be looking, in a broader sense, after its own economic interests. But South Korea's vacillation in accepting the plan has renewed Pentagon's fears over the spectre of South Korea's suppressed pro-China stance. But to allay such fears, South Korea only recently on 8 July 2016 announced that it has reached an agreement with the United States to deploy a THAAD system in Seongju, a rural town in the Gyeong-sang province of South Korea. The system is expected to be operational by the end of 2017. Why this change of heart?

North Korea's government remains defiant in the face of new harsh international sanctions imposed after its sixth nuclear test and a long-range rocket launches. China and Russia supported these new sanctions by the United Nations much to the displeasure of North Korea. Perhaps under these circumstances, North Korea may no longer submit allegiance to its two regional communist powers and decide on a unilateral aggressive action. But the most important event that most likely may have motivated South Korea to accept the anti-missile defence system was North Korea's submarine-launched ballistic missile test fired off its north-eastern region near the coastal town of Sinpo. If North Korea is successful in developing this type of offensive weaponry, then there is every reason for South Korea to heed this development and undertake the installation of the THAAD system. If China cannot rein in North Korea's nuclear ambitions, then it is prudent for South Korea to render itself relying less on China to keep North Korea at bay.

Not surprisingly, China's response to South Korea's decision was swift and strong. China does not believe the North Korean threat is the true reason for the American-initiated deployment. China asserts the true purpose of installing the THAAD with its powerful sophisticated radar system is to undermine China's own nuclear deterrence by giving the US the ability to quickly track launches of Chinese missiles. Its foreign minister, Wang Yi, has expressed the Chinese view that this deployment has disrupted the strategic balance in North-east Asia, and has added:

> The THAAD system has far exceeded the need for defence in the Korean Peninsula and will undermine the security interests of China and Russia, shatter the regional strategic balance and trigger an arms race. China understands South Korea's rational need for defence, but we cannot understand and we will not accept why they made a deployment exceeding the need.

South Korea's decision to deploy the THAAD system in Seongju has not only angered China for strategic reasons but also the very residents of the remote Korean village of 50,000. Protesters in Seoul pelted South Korea's prime minister with eggs and water bottles as he tried to allay the concerns of citizens living near the site where the US THAAD missile defence system will be deployed. They are outraged that the decision was made unilaterally without prior consultation or agreement with them. Their concerns range from becoming a military target, radiation hazard, to electromagnetic wave emissions which would produce physical stress in exposed subjects, and loss of ability to regulate body heat.

A Final Analysis

While the above opinions about China's intentions in launching the AIIB might be seen somewhat speculative, there is also the view of a lesser insidious purpose with a more pragmatic objective behind this initiative. Over the course of the last few decades China has created massive international foreign reserves approaching US$ 5 trillion in 2016. It can be argued that the AIIB was created as a means to diversify and utilise this reserve. China with its controlling interest of the bank may be more inclined to channel funds towards international infrastructure developments which would produce for China economic benefits and create new possibilities of employment for the Chinese masses by way of internationalising its labour force. Small scale examples of such benefits were realised in China's investments in African development projects employing Chinese labour and management teams. In summary, this pragmatic view of the AIIB initiative may be capsulated in China's desire to circulate its reserves for economic dividends and through its funding of Central Asian projects build the necessary infrastructure to enhance the success of the Belt and Road Initiative - the 21st century expanded equivalent of the ancient Silk Road. One final food for thought is the question whether China's dividends from operating the AIIB will promote the use of the Chinese currency - the renminbi, i.e., the yuan - instead of the US dollar in international trade?

An important counter argument to the pragmatic views presented above is the perception by many Western groups that funding and supporting infrastructure developments are not so politically neutral or economically beneficial as they are perceived. In China's case there is one looming significant pitfall. China's claim of sovereignty essentially over the entire South China Sea may turn out to be AIIB's Achilles' heel. The bank plans to award its first loans by the middle of 2016 which precedes the expected United Nations arbitration tribunal's ruling in the Hague on the Philippines' appeal against the Chinese territorial claims in the South China Sea.[2] Yet China has adamantly refused participation in this internationally assembled body in the Hague to examine the dispute on the grounds that the tribunal has no jurisdiction over sovereignty issues. China's rejection of the tribunal's role is a potential source of difficulty for the AIIB as its borrowers [may] exploit China's stance against multilateral dispute resolution protocols and renege on their loan repayment commitments. In such circumstances AIIB will lack the international support, especially from its rival the IMF, ADB and WB, for enforcing penalties and collection procedures. Will China take what it might consider appropriate precautions to secure the AIIB's loans?

No doubt China desires to convert its foreign reserves into political capital as a cushion for the need to disseminate its growing global vision. It partly emulates the US-style non-invasive foreign aid approach policy designed to extract goodwill from its clients. Countries with projects looking for development funding are expected to include Pakistan, Indonesia and possibly Iceland. But China is viewed with great scepticism hence must pursue its global objectives in a way that will not invite suspicions or cause retaliation.

South Koreans hold their national flags and banners to protest against the deployment of the Terminal High Altitude Area Defence system during a rally on 21 July 2016 in Seoul, capital of South Korea. (Korea Times).

Chapter IX

China's Muse I: Japan

Past Superiorities

The First Opium War (1839-42 CE) and the Second Opium War (1857-60 CE) launched against imperial China by Western allies had left the Chinese economy fragmented and inextricably disarrayed. The failed economy and the political turmoil that prevailed in China during the mid-19th century (1855-73 CE) gave the Muslims in the provinces of Xinjiang, Yunnan and Gansu the impetus to rebel for secession though these rebellious movements were eventually squashed and ended. But by the late 19th century the orchestrated and the organised abuse of the much weakened Chinese empire by the West had not yet run its full course. Major political and territorial concessions continued to be extracted from China by military action. In 1884 CE the French defeated the Chinese navy in the South China Sea and ended Vietnam as a Chinese colony.[1] A decade later in the First Sino-Japanese War of 1894 China suffered a humiliating defeat as the Japanese attacked and destroyed the remnants of the Chinese naval fleet at Shandong province's Weihai naval base thus giving Japan full control of the Bohai Bay in the Yellow Sea. By the terms of the ensuing Treaty of Shimonoseki China lost part of southern

Manchuria and the island of Formosa (modern Taiwan) as war reparations[2] and Korea was ceded to Japan as a protectorate.

Yet a more psychologically and socially damaging to the Chinese-Japanese relations was to come in the form of the Second Sino-Japanese War of 1937-45 CE). On 7 July 1937 Japan launched its massive invasion of China and by the end of the year had occupied Shanghai and the Republic of China's capital Nanjing (Nanking). The effects of the atrocities committed there by the Japanese soldiers that have come to be equated as 'Rape of Nanking', continue to reverberate to the present day in the minds and hearts of the Chinese populace, young and old. Millions of Chinese civilians were raped, mutilated and killed by the Japanese who piled the bodies of the massacred victims on the shores of the river Qinhuai and photographed themselves standing before them as mementoes of their triumphs. The above brief references to the troubled dark and sadly rather recent history of China and her relationship with Japan, by all means not all inclusive, unequivocally did set the tone to all subsequent Sino-Japanese relationships. Thus, tension and perpetual animosities between the two nations have constantly dogged their intercourse in the political and commercial arena. Yet, there is dichotomy to this Sino-Japanese state of affairs. The two countries are geographically separated merely by the East China Sea and Japan has in the past been strongly influenced by China in the fields of Japanese language, architecture, religion and particularly in the practice of social philosophy drawn from Confucianism. The precepts of Confucian teachings still to this day define the roots of governance in the Japanese society.

Cultural Intercourses

During the reign of the second Tang Dynasty emperor, Tai Zong (627-649 CE), the network of China's amicable and friendly economic bases extended from India and Central Asia in the west to Korea and Japan in the east.[3] The development of early sea routes out of China's Gulf of Bohai were encouraged by the Japanese trading enterprises and had given China's north-eastern Shantung (Shandong) Peninsula new and relatively conflict-free access to the Korean Peninsula. Thus Chinese merchants readily crossed the Yellow Sea to Korea and Japan to conduct their business as evidenced by archaeological finds such as a Vietnamese wooden plate with the engraved date of 1330 recovered in the northern parts of the Japanese Kyushu Island suggesting goods produced in Vietnam had reached Japan most likely through China's Shandong province. But the blossoming of this 7th century CE trade between China and Japan had to wait until the 12th century.

In the early years of the 12th century China's eastern port city of Quanzhou (also known as Chinchu or Zaytun) in Fujian province had not yet acquired the trading status enjoyed by the southern port of Guangzhou with its massive international trading establishments operating throughout the South-east Asian archipelago. Quanzhou's trading excellence developed slowly. Although Quanzhou was founded during the Tang dynasty in the second decade of the 8th century CE, its position as a major eastern port in China was not realised until the arrival of Muslim traders from India and Arabia. The trickle of Muslim traders, who arrived in Quanzhou in the 9th century as part of Tang dynasty's ambitious trade policies for expansion, became the nucleus of the Muslim communities that slowly grew and flourished in Quanzhou. These non-aggressive trade-focused Muslim communities were tolerated by the Chinese and were allowed to manage the growing commercial traffic in return for a hefty share of the profits in the form of state taxes, levies and tributes. In the centuries that followed, especially in late Song (960–1279 CE) and Yuan (1279–1368 CE) dynasties, Quanzhou became one of the world's largest seaports, and was home for a large population of foreign-born inhabitants from Europe, Middle East, India and the Pacific islands. Their chief legacy was the founding in the late 14th century (Ming dynasty) of a second sea port in Fujian province historically known as Amoy (modern Xiamen). In the mid 16th century Xiamen was used extensively by Portuguese merchants for the export of tea to Europe. However, the port became the first casualty of the First Opium War of 1839 which by virtue of the Treaty of Nanjing the port became a free zone outside China's jurisdiction. Nevertheless, historically Quanzhou in the 12th century allowed the Japanese maritime shipping to venture far away from home by first visiting the ports of Quanzhou and Xiamen then setting course to journeys across the East China and South China seas to the neutral ports of Cochin-China in the Gulf of Tonkin.

In relation to religion and music, the ancient Silk Road, discussed earlier, became the primary conduit through which Buddhism reached China.[4] Through China's long trade relationships with the Korean Peninsula across the Yellow Sea, the Buddhist faith advanced to Korea in the 4th century CE, and within the next two centuries Buddhist teachings would cross the Korean Straits from the southern tip of the peninsula and enter Japan. Even in music, tunes accompanied by lute, especially a five-stringed version of this musical instrument called the 'beewah,' or by the Arabesque string instrument known to the Chinese as 'pipa' are believed to have travelled from Kuqa (Kucha), a mostly Islamic city in north-central Xinjiang province and had crossed the Yellow Sea unsurprisingly and then crossing the Korean Straits had reached Japan. Much of this musical tradition had found great favour in the ancient imperial Japanese courts.

But by the mid 19th century the political fortunes of China under the rule of the Manchu-led dynasty looked bleak and continued to deteriorate at an accelerated rate. The economic development of the traditional Chinese agrarian society had come to a halt as a consequence of the limitations of its own man-powered pre-industrial mode of production devoid of modern mechanizations. Furthermore, the threat to China's development and industrialisation became imminent as Japan's interests in expansionism across the East China Sea were taking form.

War and Peace

Japan's pacifist constitution enacted on 3 May 1947, after Japan was defeated in World War II, was heralded as a key accomplishment of the American victory in the Pacific theatre under General Douglas MacArthur and became famous for Japan's renunciation of the right to wage future wars. However, the notion of Japan's renunciation of war as an instrument of national policy became tenuous after the establishment of the People's Republic of China in 1949 under the leadership of Chairman Mao Tse Tung. The rapid political and economic changes that have taken place in China since the communist takeover in 1949 have totally re-written the script of the Sino-Japanese relationship.

Soon after the end of World War II the United States began earnestly the reconstruction of Japan and the two nations quickly became allies and on the backs of the mighty American military they set out to project a semblance of military stability in the Pacific Rim. Yet this notion of stability in the Far East, subject to American hegemony, took a rapid turn to oblivion precisely because of the end of the war. Japan had annexed the Korean Peninsula in 1910 and the peninsula had remained under the suzerainty of Japan until Japan's defeat in the Second World War. With the end of the war it became clear that the allies would have to take over the administration of Japan and its former colonies. While the US assumed the responsibility of administering Japan and the Philippine Islands, the communist-led Soviet Union wasted no time in taking over the control of the northern sectors of the Korean Peninsula. For the Russians this was simply an opportunity to recover lands that Tsar Nicholas II's government had relinquished to Imperial Japan after the Russo-Japanese War of 1904-05. Since the end of the Sino-Japanese War of 1895, Russia had continually sought a warm-water base for a year-round operation of its navy for which Russia had leased Port Arthur (Lushun) in Liaodong Peninsula from China. China harbouring deep rooted resentments of Japan was more than pleased to accommodate the Russian navy. With Russia's threat of its navy at Port Arthur, Russia had demanded that Korea north of 39th parallel should be demilitarised and that Imperial Japanese forces should withdraw south. But Japan weary of Russia's expansionist strategy had offered to recognise Russian suzerainty over Manchuria in exchange of Russia's recognition of Japan's suzerainty over Korea. Having failed to reach an agreement, Japan began hostilities by a surprise attack on Russia's navy berthed at Port Arthur.

The logistical conflicts between the US and the Soviet Union regarding the administration of Japan's former possession, the Korean Peninsula, and whether that administration should be conducted entirely by a communist-led government, or by a non-communist democratically elected government, precipitated a massive mistrust between the Russians in the north and the Americans in the south. This resulted in the affirmation of a demarcation line along the 38th parallel, formally proposed by Dean Rusk and his colleague Charles Bonesteel which divided the peninsula into communist north and anti-communist south.

The current impasse concerning the North Korea's place in the family of nations is a many-faceted political chess game between the US and China. Clearly China needs a stable North Korea as its southern neighbour but at the same time North Korea is a tool for China to exasperate the West with its preoccupation with the nuclear threat that North Korea poses internationally. Often North Korea has responded to Western carrots for curbing its nuclear ambitions but they are perhaps only political tactics to lead the West into believing that the staunchly secretive beleaguered communist country is indeed in desperate need of social assistance. The perceived despot in North Korea's ruler with his occasional defectors is wrongly seen by the West as a man holding a nation desperately balanced on the edge of a precipice. The country's massive nuclear programmes seem to go on unabated at a level that belies not only the West's belief in the suffering of the Korean people but also how such an economically strapped nation can maintain nuclear programmes that many other freely trading countries would find impossible to undertake without serious social consequences and economic collapse. Therefore, the serious question is: How does North Korea maintain its status quo despite the massive retaliatory economic measures taken by the West?

It should not go amiss that every morning from the Chinese port city of Dandong goods-laden trucks - with grain, machinery, electronics, medicine, Petroleum products, etc. - rumble across the narrow bridge over the Yalu River inching their way into North Korea. The trucks and the goods within them unequivocally represent North Korea's manufacturing and economic lifeline. China is the only country left that is openly willing to do significant trade with its communist neighbour. China is North Korea's only major ally, and accounts for more than 70% of North Korea's total trade volume. Although China helped draft United Nation's new tougher sanction guidelines, and said it will vigorously implement them, there is little evidence showing China intends to comply. Moreover, China in the past has been criticised for not enforcing previous sanctions.

There is no doubt China intends to maintain its profile as a global superpower. Its political influence over North Korea has been a tool for the Chinese who have used it to confound and bewilder the Western allies into a defensive position. China will therefore strive to preserve stability in North Korea if for no other reason than to reduce the possibility of a US-backed Japanese pre-emptive strike against North Korea in an effort to prevent Japan from constantly being a certain nuclear target for North Korea. No doubt such a pre-emptive military strike would ultimately imply deployment and the presence of US/Japanese boots in North Korean territories directly along the north-eastern borders of China. This scenario would be unacceptable to China as it would produce three monumental consequences for it. First, the presence of US-backed military presence at China's doorsteps is a major strategic disadvantage to China's security and bargaining power in international circles with a clear loss of clout and assertiveness that have characterised China's foreign policies in recent years. The second consequence is that neutralisation of North Korea's nuclear programme nullifies China's self-serving manipulative tactics in international politics based on North Korean nuclear programmes. A third consequence, which will certainly bring much internally demographic problems and economic instability within China, may result from massive refugees pouring across the Yalu River from the dismantled North Korean social order which cannot be viewed as acceptable in light of China's global ambitions. These three consequences would be so devastating to China's emergence as a proud and a confident superpower that China would be compelled to defend North Korea militarily against any and all Western/Japanese or South Korean military operations.

Currently China and Japan are on the opposite side of several regional issues ranging from territorial disputes to economic competition. Despite past reconciliatory efforts championed by both countries, such as the normalisation of the Sino-Japanese relations signed on 29 September 1972, the Treaty of Peace and Friendship between Japan and the People's Republic of China signed on 12 August 1978[5] and the Official Development

Assistance to China from Japan which began in 1979, many conflicts and vital self-interest issues have plagued these two nations.[6] China and Japan have been at war with each other a number of times since 1894[7] and the likelihood of a future war is not out of the realm of possibilities should diplomacy fail. And if past human derelictions in peace efforts are used as indicators for avoiding future catastrophes, diplomacy will most certainly leave the world community wanting.

Chapter X

China's Muse II: North Korea

Re-visiting the Treaty of Friendship

In July 2011, Chinese Deputy Premier Zhang De Jiang travelled to Pyongyang to celebrate the 50th anniversary of the *Treaty of Friendship, Cooperation and Mutual Assistance* signed on 11 July 1961 by the first premier of People's Republic of China, Zhou En Lai, and Kim Il-Sung, the founder of the Democratic People's Republic of Korea, otherwise known as North Korea, thus binding the two nations together in a bilateral military alliance which remains in force to the present day and with a recent extension will remain in effect until 2021. Although this alliance is merely an instrument for political operations, it expresses little of the unspoken reality of the long abiding cultural and social ties that have existed for millennia between the peoples of China and the Korean Peninsula. Article 2 of the treaty states a mutual defence provision and reads as follows:

> The contracting parties undertake jointly to adopt all measures to prevent aggression against either of the contracting parties by any state. In the event of one of the contracting parties being subjected to the armed attack by

any state or several states jointly and thus being involved in a state of war, the other contracting party shall immediately render military and other assistance by all means at its disposal.

The essence of the friendship treaty is reflected as a typical asymmetric security alliance by which the stronger party provides security assistance to the weaker party while the weaker party accepts restrictions to its independent military activities. However, asymmetric alliances are froth with complications especially when clashes of national interests gradually begin to raise their ugly heads, or more significantly, when the weaker party begins aggressively to pursue a deliberate course of increasing its own military potency. And herein lies the Chinese current dilemma with North Korea.

China and North Korea are bound by Article 1 of the friendship treaty whose declarative clause requires pledging efforts by the contracting parties for the protection of world peace and security of all nations. Furthermore, Article 4 of the treaty also requires the contracting parties to maintain continual mutual consultation on all important international issues of common interest. The difficulty for China in dealing productively and effectively with North Korea arose when the Cold War ended in 1992 and China and South Korea bilaterally agreed to normalise their relationship and establish formal diplomatic ties. China's action in this context was apparently no more than a deliberate pursuit of its own global interests. Consequently, to the North Koreans, the significance of their friendship treaty with China lost much of its lustre. North Korea was angered by this normalisation as it directly impacted negatively on its sworn mission for the unification of the peninsula.

It is clear that since the end of the Korean War and the signing of the armistice agreement in 1953, North Korea has felt threatened by the United States and Japan, and has always feared an invasion by a US-South Korean alliance. Therefore, after China normalised its relationship with South Korea, it was expected that North Korea would choose to march to the tunes of its own drum beat but surprisingly it did not terminate the friendship treaty with China, presumably, as a safety net should it required the assistance of China in future years. But the mould was cast and fractures began to appear - or did they? - in the China-North Korea asymmetric alliance. It is hard not to be cynical about the advantages that China would reap from its normalised relationship with the South. This can be promoted in the international arena as *fait accompli* in China's loss of reasonable control of North's external political affairs yet remaining able to provide the North Koreans with economic and military support. Also, in view of the fact that China-North Korea friendship treaty is a mutually binding defence instrument, China can remain a deterrent force against any attempt by any state to pre-emptively and militarily attack North Korea. No doubt this is a cleverly drawn strategy consistent with China's schemes for keeping the United States and its allies at an arm's length from China's sovereign borders, and also potentially indirectly preventing an overwhelming dominance of the Pacific Rim by the US military which might be seen as detrimental to China's global posture. Will China intervene in defence of North Korea in the event of an external attack on North Korea? The international community is of the opinion that China opposes both nuclear proliferation and war in the Korean peninsula. Beijing will not encourage any party to stir up military conflict and will firmly resist any change to China's *status quo* in areas where China's interests are threatened.

Chapter XI

China's Muse III: Taiwan

The Crux of the Issue

The Chinese communist government's willingness to establish diplomatic relations with the United States began in February 1972 with President Richard Nixon's visit to Beijing. This visit produced the *Shanghai Communiqué* which in effect was an acknowledgement by China and the US that the two nations would strive to normalise their relationship despite their mutual concerns regarding the political status of the island of Taiwan. The concerns stemmed from the fact that both Beijing and the government of Taiwan agreed there was only 'One China' and that Taiwan was in fact a part of the 'One China' principle. However, difficulties in moving forward with the normalisation of relations with the US began to surface when both the communist government of the People's Republic of China and the nationalist Republic of China claimed to be the legitimate government of China. The nationalist Republic of China was the government of mainland China established in 1912 after the fall of the Qing dynasty in 1911. Following their loss in the Chinese civil war in 1949, the nationalists withdrew to Taiwan under the command of Chiang Kai Shek but continued to claim to represent the legitimate government of China.

The government of the Republic of China continued to represent China at the United Nations assembly until 1971, when the People's Republic of China took over the China seat, causing the republic to lose its United Nation membership. Without further arguments on the political status of Taiwan at this point, perhaps it will suffice to say that Taiwan's claim of its government being the legitimate government of all China cannot be reasonably accepted given the declaration made by the United Nations general assembly in favour of the People's Republic. Justifiably, Beijing soon thereafter took the position that the matter of Taiwan was an internal matter for China to deal with, and that the US or any other nation should not interfere. Agreeably, the US terminated its formal ties with Taiwan in support of the 'One China' principle.

The matter of Taiwan would have been settled amicably between the US and China had it not been for US's decision to open independent channels of communication with Taiwan thus overshadowing the principle of 'One China.' Chiang Kai Shek ruled Taiwan under authoritarian single party regime until 1979 when human rights protests succeeded in establishing democratic rule in the island. Unfortunately at this juncture in Taiwan's history, the US Congress saw fit to pass the *Taiwan Relations Act* which sought to provide Taiwan with military hardware and defence services despite the fact that the island was no longer a sovereign state. One may argue that this was a small gesture by the United States to guarantee the security of Taiwan's people, though the US had no moral right to do so, the true reason was to maintain American credibility as the force for peace in Asia. Once the floodgates of military assistance to Taiwan were opened, further armaments and of their improved updated sophisticated versions continued to flow robustly into Taiwan, implying the US was pursuing a 'Two China' policy for its own global interests. Although China offered Taiwan the option of internal autonomy by a 'One Country, Two Systems' framework analogous to that offered by Deng Xiao

Ping to Hong Kong in 1997 and subsequently to Macao in 1997, the Taiwanese summarily dismissed the offer as too risky and unreliable, anchoring this decision on the strength of their alliance with the United States. From Beijing's viewpoint, the United States seemed to have violated all earlier international determinations regarding China's sovereignty over Taiwan but, not surprisingly, Beijing elected to adhere to the practice of the familiar adage, 'There is more than one way to skin a cat,' firmly believing that the US will not spill American blood in defence of Taiwan as it had fruitlessly for a decade or more in Vietnam. Beijing felt secure in this belief thus threatened the use of military force against Taiwan in response to any formal declaration of independence. Beijing was biding its time.

Taiwan from the 17th to the 20th Century

A brief summary of the relevant history of Taiwan is given here to aid the reader in following the arguments that follow. It is to be noted that in 1626, the Spanish Empire occupied northern Taiwan as a base to extend their trading.[1] The Spanish colonial period in Taiwan lasted sixteen years until 1642, when the last Spanish fortress fell to Dutch forces. A self-styled Ming dynasty loyalist named Zheng Cheng Gong, attacked the island in 1662 putting an end to the Dutch military occupation of the island. Zheng and his heirs ruled Taiwan from 1662 to 1682 with their occasional raids on the southeast coast of mainland China against the Qing dynasty that had deposed the Ming dynasty.[2] In 1683 Admiral Shi Lang of southern Fujian province vanquished the last Ming heir in Taiwan thus the Qing dynasty formally annexed Taiwan and placed it under the jurisdiction of Fujian province in south-east mainland China. As the Qing dynasty was defeated in the First Sino-Japanese War (1894–1895), Taiwan was ceded in full sovereignty to the Empire of Japan by the Treaty of Shimonoseki of 17 April 1895.

The proprietary rights of the island of Taiwan, like many other colonised Asiatic islands by the West, is beguiling in the sense that the question of its rightful ownership depends on one's view on ownership. So, would it be correct to suggest that modern Italy is the rightful owner of England as the Roman Empire was once the masters of Britain? Likewise, would it be correct to suggest that modern Spain is the rightful owner of the Central Americas as the Spanish once dominated the Meso-Americas, or for the same reason should it claim ownership of the Island of Taiwan, or rather should the Dutch claim ownership of Taiwan? The history of human civilisation amply demonstrates unequivocally that the most recent masters of a land, possessed either by force or treaty, become its rightful owners. World history is peppered with such examples, such as the taking of Northern Ireland by King Edward I of England; the winning of Palestine by Israel; and the extreme example is the defeat of the empire of Japan in 1945 by the allies, yet by treaty reverting the possession of the Japanese islands to its people. One might ask what is the point? Following the Japanese surrender to the allies in 1945, the Republic of China took control of Taiwan not as owners or conquerors of the island but simply as interim administrative body under the command of General Chen Yi who was ferried to the island along with his forces by the US navy.

The Republic of China which was established in 1912 in mainland China ceased to exist after the communist victory in the Chinese civil war of 1949 henceforth all its claims of land ownerships including Taiwan, and with their loss to the communist, the Republic of China thus had completely *forfeited its right to exercise state sovereignty on behalf of all China.* Moreover, the continued presence of the nationalists in Taiwan until the loss of their United Nations seat in 1971 is tantamount to the diminutive term 'squatting.' Under these circumstances, would it not be correct to assume that the *Treaty of Taipai,* orchestrated by the Supreme Commander for the Allied Powers and signed by Japan under duress on 28 April 1952 that seceded Taiwan to the nationalists, was nothing less than a self-serving hasty replacement of the *Treaty of San Francisco* of September 1951 that had failed to grant the nationalists sovereignty over Taiwan? Is it a surprise, therefore, that the *Treaty of Taipei* was abrogated unilaterally by the Japanese government on 29 September 1972?[3]

The current speculation in some circles that China plans sometime in the future to invade Taiwan militarily[4] utterly fails to take into account the well-honed Chinese common-sense which has been practiced over centuries. The notion that China will one day attack Taiwan is a premise without merit as the action would summarily draw the Chinese into a military confrontation with the United States. Why would China take such a foolish step risking its planned and well executed gains in the global political and economic theatres? Perhaps the coveted internationally recognised sovereignty of China over Taiwan in this instance is less relevant to China than the reality of China's overt domination of the Taiwanese economic strength in which the United States is less able to influence on account of China's generational bonds with the Chinese populace of Taiwan and of their common heritage usually referred to as *tongwen; tongzhong* – that is same culture, same race. One does not need to go very far to observe Chinese diaspora's loyalty to mainland China as evidenced by their individual unbroken family links and economic connections.

More than One Way to Skin a Cat

Since Taiwan's ruling nationalist party ousted the island's Democratic Progressive Party's candidate in Taiwan's presidential polls in 2008, its political tensions with China had significantly subsided especially as Taiwan's then newly elected nationalist president Ma Ying Jeou had accepted China's position that relations between the two countries should be based on the

'1992 consensus'; namely that Taiwan accepts there is but one China, despite of their desperate interpretations of the meaning of the word consensus. This acceptance of the '1992 consensus' has played a critical role in boosting Taiwan's cross-strait economic ties, and according to recent statistical reports their cross-strait trade volume had reached nearly US$ 100 billion in the first seven months of 2016. A major portion of the enhanced economic ties is significantly reflected in the large-scale Taiwanese investments in mainland China and by the large number of Chinese Taiwanese employed in the industrial sectors along China's south-eastern provinces of Guangdong, Fujian and Zhejiang. Moreover, China's premier, Li Ke Qiang has repeatedly reasserted the importance of both the 'One China' principle and the '1992 consensus' in protecting the interests of Taiwanese investors. Uncertainties in Taiwan's massive investments within China can impede Taiwan's future trade potential and make it more difficult for Taiwan to sign free-trade agreements with other countries. Taiwan is also aware of the economic benefits it can amass from participating in the regional economic integration initiative launched by Beijing in the form of the Asian Infrastructure Investment Bank (AIIB). Although Taiwan is eager to join AIIB as a founding member, Beijing has stated that joining will be welcome as long as Taiwan joined under the 'One China' principle. It is likely that Taiwan's level of economic integration with China will ultimately become the moving force for the formal unification of the two countries on China's terms.

Taiwan: Root of Phantom Expectations

The posture taken by the United States as an ally and defender of Taiwan is a major obstacle on the hopeful road to developing a truly unencumbered cooperative relationship with China. It is not unlikely that the Chinese consider the American commitments to maintaining peace in the Pacific region simply a front to contain China's global leadership and prevent it from becoming a major opposition force challenging the American military-based universal hegemony.

Taiwan is the cornerstone of China-US relationship and of the peace and stability desired in the region. To challenge Beijing's 'One China' policy is problematic and to the detriment of Taiwan. Although Taiwan's younger generation strives for stable independent democratic self-rule on the island, it is more likely that Taiwan's administrators see the future security of the island in the 'One China' policy.

Throughout recent sales of arms to Taiwan, particularly under Presidents Bush Sr., Clinton and as late as President Trump, the US has maintained a substantial arms delivery programme to Taiwan despite China's opposition and displeasure. In September of 1992, the Bush Administration sent a top State Department official to Beijing to explain the president's decision to reverse ten years of American policy on Taiwan and permit the sale of offensive F-16 warplanes to Taiwan. Even if this sale does not violate the 1982 arms communiqué worked out between the US and China, the mere physical action of providing Taiwan with offensive military hardware without China's involvement is a direct denouncement of the 'One China' policy. This type of American collusion with Taiwan was also seen in the Clinton Administration years when the Pentagon forged strategic planning with Taiwan's arms forces. To add insult to injury, in June of 2017 the Trump Administration notified Congress of its plans to go ahead with the controversial arms package to Taiwan totalling the enormous sum of US$ 1.42 billion which would provide Taiwan with missiles, torpedoes and electronics. Not unexpectedly, the Chinese embassy in Washington complained this sale grossly interferes in China's domestic affairs under its 'One China' policy and erodes the trust of cooperation and the consensus reached between Presidents Trump and Xi Jin Ping at their meeting in Mar A Lago, Florida. What should be China's reaction to such provocations and assault on its 'One China' policy short of creating a massive political fallout and potential physical conflict that will harm its continued 'apparent' self-serving amicable relationship with the US? There is, perhaps, one potential answer.

In the imaginary event that North Korea succeeds in detonating a nuclear warhead above Honolulu, the blast would eliminate the city and the massive US military base at Pearl Harbour resulting in the crippling of US's Pacific forces to a degree the Japanese could not have hoped to achieve in 1941. Undoubtedly, the sole winner would be China — not even a principal party to the conflict. Could this be the reason why Beijing pretends to vacillate about not helping the US halt North Korea's nuclear programmes?

Washington deludes itself by desperately arguing that its concern over our security and that of the nations at large will make China discard its trump card that holds the US in virtual captivity. A US-led pre-emptive strike against North Korea is unthinkable based on the potential instantaneous losses of the Japanese and South Korean civilisations. Hence, business is as usual. Washington's undeclared undermining of the 'One China' policy and violating China's sovereignty over Taiwan will continue to confound the US military and policymakers on how to deal with North Korea. It is the proverbial thorn inflicting pain, but in the present context, covertly to those who appear to be China's enemies. Recalling Sun Tzu's remark: 'The supreme art of war is to subdue the enemy without fighting' or 'If you are far from the enemy, make him believe you are near.'

Table IV: Summary of Text Statistics

Topic	Country	Date	Value	Page___
Gross domestic product (GDP)	China	2010	US$	6 Trillion
Projected GDP	China	2020	US$	12 Trillion
GDP	China	2016	US$	> 12 Trillion
Gross domestic product (GDP)	China	1978	US$	217 Billion
		2015	US$	>11 Trillion
Private sector's share of GDP/capita	China	1978	US$	227
		2015	US$	8,280
Trade balance with China	Canada	2014	C$	-28.6 Billion
		2015	C$	-34.3 Billion
Trade balance with the USA	China	1985	US$	+6 Million
		2015	US$	+340 Billion
Outstanding public debt	USA	2016	US$	19 Trillion
Debt owed to China	USA	2016	US$	1.3 Trillion
Trade with ASEAN	China	2003	US$	60 Billion
		2008	US$	193 Billion
Trade with Africa	China	2000	US$	10 Billion
		2014	US$	200 Billion
Public's opinion on their nation's direction		China	85% (positive)	
		USA	26%	
Public's opinion on standard of living higher than 5 years ago		China	73%	
		USA	27%	
Public's opinion future holds promise for next generation		China	82% (positive)	
		USA	33%	
Public's optimism level		China	93% (positive)	
		USA	Low	

Notes

Chapter I

1. J. G. Ghazarian 2014, p. 8. 'tian-xia' Land under the Heaven, mostly considered to be the north-central and eastern provinces of present-day China.
2. Mao Tse Tung 1967, pp. 30-34. Under the heading of Vanguards of the Revolution, the report delineates how the poor peasants have always been the main force in the bitter fight in the countryside. It concludes that the poor peasants have been the most responsive to the Communist Party leadership.
3. Mao Tse Tung 1967, pp. 13-19. The 'Analysis' defines the Landlords as wholly the appendage of the international bourgeoisie. The Middle Bourgeoisie is the Capitalist class. The Petty Bourgeoisie class is represented by the master craftsmen, students, primary and secondary school teachers, lower governmental functionaries, office clerks and minor privately practicing layers. The Semi Proletariat class is composed of semi-owner and tenanted peasants who made up a large portion of the rural classes. Also included in this class are the shop assistants and peddlers.

Chapter II

1. M Mamdani 2004, p. 32. Perhaps a clearer insight into Orientalism can be gained from the seminal work titled *Orientalism* by Edward W. Said, first published in 1978, which reviews the history of Western perceptions of the East and renders these perceptions as a powerful European ideological tool used by all Europeans particularly the colonial administrators who were engaged with the social fabric of the East and dealt with the unfamiliar Eastern traditional cultural practices.
2. M. Leonard 2008, p. 9. It tells us about the kind of society China is and wants to become.

Chapter III

1. M. R. McNeilly 2001, p. 5.
2. R. D. Sawyer 2007, p. 23.
3. *ibid*, pp. 38-39.
4. H. J. *Van de Ven 2000, pp. 6-7.*
5. R. D. Sawyer 2007, pp. 113-116.
6. K.W. Chase *2003, p. 15.*
7. I. Galambos 2011, pp. 80-82
8. J. Needham 1995, pp. 15-20.
9. C. M. Gyves 1993, pp. 16-18. In recent times the Chinese armed forces seem to have expanded their list of study of classic Chinese personalities to include the statesman and philosopher Shang Yang (c.390-338 BCE) who emphasised the role of the military in his economic theories.

Chapter IV

1. F. B. Gibney 2012, p 44.
2. Data and Statistics 2015.
3. A. Wagstaff et al. 2009, pp.1-19.

Chapter V

1. Cited from Global Indicators Database of Pew Research Centre - Global Attitudes and Trends.
2. A. Lamb 1966.
3. J. S. Goldstein 1997, pp. 30–31.
4. J. B. Calvin 1984.
5. Suzerainty (as defined online) is an artificially formed word derived from the late 18th-century word suzerain. It was first used to refer to the dominant position of the Ottoman Empire in relation to its surrounding regions; the Ottoman Empire being the *suzerain*, and the relationship being *suzerainty*. The terminology gradually became generalised to refer to any relationship in which one region or people controls the foreign policy and international relations of a tributary state, while allowing the tributary nation to have internal autonomy. Modern writers also sometimes use the term *suzerain* to refer to a feudal lord, in regard to their relationship to their vassals.
6. A. Lamb 1964, pp. 144-5.
7. T. Shakya 1999, pp. 279-85.
8. D. Woodman 1969, pp 1-22.
9. *ibid.*
10. N. Maxwell 1970, pp 20-35.
11. *ibid.*
12. K. Gupta 1971, No. 47, pp. 521-45.
13. N. Maxwell 1970, pp. 384-470.
14. P. B. Sinha et al. 1962.
15. N. Maxwell 1970, pp. 47-80.

Chapter VI

1. Data approved by the Ministry of Public Works and Government Services Canada.
2. Source: United States Census Bureau, Foreign Trade.
3. R. Gilpin 1988, pp. 591-613.

4. J. S. Goldstein 2005, p. 107.
5. M. L. Weidenbaum 1996, pp. 4-8.
6. C. W. Freeman, Jr. 2010, 20 January.
7. D. Bandow 2017, p. 13.
8. World Steel Association, *World Steel in Figures.* 2010, p.8.

Chapter VII

1. E. L. Dreyer 2006.
2. M. Riegl, et al. 2014, pp. 66-68. Two 'dashes' from the original eleven were removed in the early 1950s to bypass the Gulf of Tonkin as a gesture of communist solidarity with China's comrades in North Vietnam.
3. United Nations Convention on the Law of the Sea treaty (UNCLOS) was opened for signature on 10 December 1982 and entered into force on 16 November 1994. The treaty which was ratified by 167 nation-states established a system of property rights concerning sea fishing activities and for mineral extraction from deep sea beds.
4. H. Cooper 2016, pp.1 & 5.
5. J. Cochrane 2016, p. 3.

Chapter VIII

1. *'UK announces plans to join Asian Infrastructure Investment Bank.' HM Treasury. 12 March 2015.*
2. The appeal by the Philippines filed with the Hague tribunal has been backed principally by the United States, the United Kingdom, France and Japan. In contrast, China has received the support of Russia, Saudi Arabia, Niger, Afghanistan and the Pacific island- nations of Togo and Vanuatu. The Philippines contests China's claims, specifically on nearby islands it says are part of the West Philippines Sea. Manila has argued that China has exceeded its entitlement under the UNCLOS treaty which

gives China 20 kilometres of territorial waters around islands it controls, far less than claimed under the nine-dash line. However, the Philippines ignores the fact that the area defined by the nine-dash line and controlled by China precedes the 1982 UNCLOS treaty by more than three decades during which there had been no recorded claimants or objections to the control. Hence, China follows a historical precedent set by the nine-dash line that the Republic of China drew in 1947 following the surrender of Japan at the end of World War II.

Chapter IX

1. O. Chapuis 1995.
2. J.E. Hoare 1995.
3. Q. Wang 2008.
4. J.G. Ghazarian 2014, pp. 215-219.
5. Article 2, 'the Contracting Parties declare that neither of them should seek hegemony in the Asia-Pacific region or any other region and that each is opposed to efforts by any other country or group of countries to establish such hegemony.'
6. I. Nish 1990, pp. 601-623.
7. L. Hagström 2008, pp. 223-40.

Chapter XI

1. J. E. Borao 2009.
2. T. Andrade 2013.
3. *International Law* [No. 25]. 1982 states it must be construed that the Treaty of Peace between Japan and the Republic of China should lose its significance of existence and come to an end through the normalisation of diplomatic relation between Japan and the People's Republic of China based on the Joint Communiqué.
4. I. Easton 2017.

Dynasties of ancient and imperial China

PERIOD	SUB-PERIOD	TIME SCALE
Ancient		
Xia (Methological)		c 2205 -1766 BC
Shang		c 1600 -1027
Zhou	Western	1027 - 771
	Eastern	770 - 256
	Spring-Autumn	772 - 481
	Warring States	475 - 221
Imperial		
Qin		221 - 206
Han	Western (Former) Han	BC 206 - 8 AD
Wang Meng userpurs		9 - 24
Han	Eastern (Later) Han	25 - 220
Three Kingdoms	Wei	220 - 265
	Shu	221 - 263
	Wu	222 - 280
Western Jin		265 - 316
Eastern Jin		317 - 420
Southern kingdoms	Song	420 - 479
	Qi	479 - 502
	Liang	502 - 557
	Chen	557 - 589
Northern kingdoms	Northern Wei	386 - 534
	Eastern Wei	534 - 550
	Northern Qi	550 - 577
	Western Wei	535 - 556
	Northern Zhou	557 - 581
Sui		581 - 618
Tang		618 - 907

Five Dynasties	Later Liang	907 - 923
	Later Tang	923 - 936
	Later Jin	936 - 947
	Later Han	947 - 950
	Later Zhou	951 - 960
Song	Northern	960 -1127
	Southern	1127 -1279
Jin (Jurchen)		1115 -1234
Yuan (Mongol)		1279 -1368
Ming		1368 -1644
Qing (Manchu)		1644 -1911
Modern		
Republic of China		1911 -1949
People's Republic of China		1949– Present

Postscript

*Those who fail to learn from history
are doomed to repeat it.*

Sir Winston Churchill, 1948

Where is China Heading?

Dystopic oblivion - and I shall qualify my answer below based
on my two decades of travelling to China since the early 2000s
in the capacity of an academic writer. My keen observations of
what has been taking place in China during the past five years
make me uncomfortable and leave me much concerned.

China's current President Xi Jin Ping's subtle, low profile
and the deliberately orchestrated approach to inculcate the
minds of his country's youth a sense of Chinese pride and
nationalism, and the return to the roots, in my opinion of their
overvalued and misrepresented ancient Chinese civilisation, are
all dangerous and do not bode well for the future of China. His
words reverberate with the echoes of China's past emperors, and
resonate with his clarion call for the *great rejuvenation of the old
Chinese civilisation.'* But, unfortunately, those who have taken
to their hearts this delusional nationalism are the street thugs,
the unemployed university drop-outs, the idle youth surviving
by illegal activities and the disenfranchised self-proclaimed
idealists who shout with anger at Western visitors of China *'Go
back where you come from; you are not wanted here. This is China.'*
The heaping of angered vulgarity and finger pointing just short
of a physical abuse are examples of their lack of civility and
politeness and emphasises the prevailing rudeness with focus

on their own personal gratification. These are problematic for a society that proclaims itself civilised and which has described its opponents in the distant past as 'Barbarians.' Ironically, I have witnessed the reverse, and I beg to differ with my countrymen who in their fervent writings suggest China is the new rising star of the millennium.

There is no confusion on President Xi's autocratic political agendas. In his most recent strongly nationalistic closing address to the National People's Congress on 11 March, he secured the blessings of the Congress with the unquestionable support of Politburo's Standing Committee to abolish the constitutional two-term limit on the presidency that gave him the power to rule indefinitely thus raising the spectre of the return to 'one-man-rule.' This achievement cannot be divorced from his aggressive remarks, most likely addressed to the United States, that 'Only those who are accustomed to threatening others will look at everyone else as threats. In the face of national righteousness and the tide of history, all attempts or tricks aimed at dividing the motherland are doomed to failure, and all will receive the condemnation of the people and the punishment of history.' He vowed China '…will take our due place in the world, and was ready to fight bloody battles against our enemies.' He further stressed that the Chinese people '…have the will and the ability to foil all activities intended to divide the nation, and are united in their belief that every inch of their great motherland cannot be and absolutely will not be separated.' Further in his speech, Mr. Xi invoked China's historical achievements in governance and culture, and stressed the importance of national unity as it strove to reach new goals in poverty alleviation. Needless to say, no one would have dared to question what Xi meant by China's historical achievements in governance and culture. I suspect he may have had in mind only the occasional limited suspension of China's oppressive everlasting feudal system in the face of its historically repeated periods of disunity and fragmentation. His clever reference to culture begs the question, whose culture did he mean, the nomadic Mongolic Yuan Dynasty that ruled China in the 13th century, or of the Bourgeois feudal land owners of many past centuries – the parasites of Western imperialism - that subjugated its people in perpetual poverty, or of the privileged minority elite of the royal courts that enjoyed opulent lives at the expense of the suffering masses? Is it a surprise that the inbred mentality of the Chinese masses throughout history has been focused, first and foremost, on individual self-preservation? After 2,000 years of Chinese history devoid of humanism, their age-old practice of Me-ism pokes out its ugly face today in the Chinese masses everywhere and in all manners – in the rush to get a seat anywhere without regard to civility or courtesy, in the use of lifts, placing an order at McDonald's or KFC, blatant jumping of queues in airport security queues, in boarding buses, etc. – which all seem to the Western traveller rather annoying and potentially unnerving. I can only suggest that analogous to these instinctive behaviours demonstrated by the Chinese masses are characteristically seen in Western television shows relating to behavioural studies of animals in the wild especially at times of sharing a kill. Now I ask: who is the Barbarian? Is this the China President Xi Jin Ping strives to present to the world, or is it a product of his policies that manifest greater political repression within an already highly controlled polity? There is little doubt that such primordial societal behaviour witnessed today in China may one day evolve to encompass the Chinese attitudes in international and foreign affairs.

As a complement to my remarks above, it is now appropriate to review the meaning of China's ancient civilisation. This civilisation, often the pride of China's youth, offered comfortable, luxurious and a controlling power to the members of the royal courts, to the elites and to the wealth-oriented families with large land holdings that were tended by feudal surfs. True, there where a few social commentators and old sages who offered their words of wisdom for the betterment of the Chinese society. Confucian Analects, the writings of Mencius, Lao Zi, Gao Zi and many others of ancient China are valued examples but the Chinese masses during the glory centuries of China still remained illiterate, primitive, mercilessly subjugated by their utterly stratified overlords and lived in rampant poverty either amongst crowded rat infested city quarters, or mostly in agrarian landscapes. But, most of all, we must remain cognizant of the truth that these human masses were the descendants of nomadic pastoralist Mongolic tribes, or of Turkic steppe peoples of Central Asia and Tibet. They included the Mongolic Xiongnu and the Xianbei Tuoba tribes, and the Tangut who were mostly related to the Tibetan Qiang tribe. Nomadic tribal traditions cannot be construed to form the foundations of a rooted civilisation. Conquered lands by the nomads were traditionally neither organised nor administered; instead they were plundered and left devastated before the conquerors returned to their nomadic tents either in the wide-open pasture lands or on the periphery of the Gobi Desert. Where was their sense of administration, the creation and application of social order, rules for civility and the respect of the rights of their fellowmen? In short, rule by nomadic hordes, the invention of gunpowder, the weaving of silk, the techniques of manufacturing exquisite pottery inherited from the early Persian merchants who brought the art to China, or the Confucian writings which addressed mostly the elite of his time, or even the words of a few sages and poets, I submit, do not define what is construed as 'civilisation' especially when there is lack of emphasis on humanism or of the uniform application of the rule of law to an all-inclusive civil society. The youth of today's China should not be misled into a false sense of pride and overconfidence. Rather than appealing to their emotional insecurities in order to instil in their collective conscience a message of superiority and hope, the sad truths of their bygone histories, the record of their human serfdom, the wealth-oriented stratification of their society that had crushed notions of individualism in the poor should be the focus of

China's political progress and the promotion of an egalitarian society. After all, was this not the sacred objective of Mao Tse Tung's Communist Revolution? Would he not find the present enormous economic gulf between the rich and the poor a repulsive *déjà vu* of a bygone era and a betrayal of his dreams for the people of China?

And, here is a demonstration of the meaning of a true civilisation – our Western civilisation. Throughout Western history, the focus of the makers of our Western civilisation was singularly and categorically society oriented – towards a general humanism, towards the creation of beauty for all to enjoy in science, art, architecture and music and a clear emphasis on individualism and human rights. The list of the makers of our civilisation is indeed very long, but here are some examples as food for thought: Socrates (pursuit of truth), Plato (civil government), Aristotle (virtue ethics), Cicero (political theory), John Wycliffe (theology and enlightenment), Thomas More (humanism), Martin Luther (theology and education), Thomas Aquinas (theology of sacrifice), Galileo Galilee (universal cosmology), René Descartes (rationalism), Voltaire (freedom of expression), Jean-Jacques Rousseau (social contract), Ludwig Wittgenstein (analysis of language), Isaac Newton (science), Charles Darwin (naturalism), Ralph Waldo Emerson (egalitarianism) and not least the Renaissance giants Michelangelo (art and beauty) and Michelangelo Caravaggio (individualism in art). In this latter context it must not escape our attention the persecution endured by the contemporary Chinese artist and activist Ai Weiwei, whose subjugation and restrains by the Chinese authorities is a sad commentary on where China is heading. The diffusion of Roman law, art and architecture into all levels of the Roman Empire are testament to the civilisation we inherited from them yet that civilisation was further complemented by the glory of the Holy Roman Empire under Charlemagne.

Today in China class stratification reminiscent of the past, albeit in modern terms, still remains wealth-dependent whilst the poverty stricken masses continue to toil in flooded rice paddies and in small plot farms lacking sanitation or life's basic necessities. And farmers, who happen to be displaced by their government's forced acquisition of their farms for the construction of roads and tower blocks, swiftly move into housings in large urbanised cities but, ironically, bring their farm-based habits along with them and create chaotic unpleasant environments devoid of any sense of community pride or of the individual rights of their neighbours. In a sense, the squalled China of yesteryears seems to perpetually dominate the ethos of the Chinese society with all its unchanging characteristics, surely a product of a civilisation that never was. So, what civilisation is there to be rejuvenated? What civilisation is there to inculcate a false and a dangerous sense of pride in China's youth? The themes now profusely aired on Chinese TV-shows are based on historical China with emphasis on ancient costumes and mannerisms. A constant flow of shows depict the struggle of the Red Armey during the Chinese civil war, or the Chinese resistance to the Japanese occupations of the 1930s that spew endless examples of synthetic bravado. Perhaps, the producers of such shows should be reminded that although nostalgia may address the objectives of the state, the world at large has moved on and no longer live with 2,000-year old ethos. Wake up China! It is a different world out there.

Is there a need to speculate on China's endgame when on television adverts a young man buries his face in an open old book with ancient Chinese writings and takes a deep exhilarating breath? Why the emphasis on a series on Confucian teachings created on the new China Educational TV? Why the focus on a spoken guided TV series on select museum exhibits of ancient Chinese artefacts, such as ceremonial ancient bronze vessels or oracular scripts of the Shang Dynasty inscribed on tortoise shells? The Orwellian 'big brother' cameras of China's Brave

New World are truly everywhere and constantly monitoring the Chinese public on foot or in public or private transports. These are regressive patterns of governance, not a paradigm of a government intent on unshackling its people from servitude.

Moreover, the Chinese state has indicated that its projected objective is a 70 to 30 percent relative distribution of its urban versus rural populations, respectively. The accelerated grabbing of farm lands evidenced across China, and forcing the masses of displaced farmers into urbanised living, as opposed to their distributions in the vastness of China's land mass, simply facilitates the state's control of its population now forced to occupy easily restrained urban quarters. Moreover, the average wait-time to dispense payments to farmers for their confiscated lands stand at the unbelievable period of 6-10 years whilst the impoverished farmers remain at the mercy of the state. In the meantime, the confiscated lands are used by the state to amass large profits from their negotiated agreements with land developers and construction companies. Yes, this is the China of today that is often privately and resignedly confessed.

Last but not least the digitized high-tech surveillance in today's China linked to personalised identification numbers is the modern version of the old conventional controls reminiscent of those used by Mao Tse Tung during the Cultural Revolution. The international repercussions of Beijing's dystopic surveillance of its people under the pretence of national security can only hurt China's bid for the world's respect and jeopardize its inclusion in the family of nations considered progressive and supportive of human rights.

Bibliography

Andrade, T. (2013) *Lost Colony: The Untold Story of China's First Great Victory over the West*. Princeton University Press, New Jersey.

Bandow, D. (2017) China is not an evil empire facing the US. in *China Daily, European Weekly*, October 6-12.

Borao, J. E. (2009) *The Spanish Experience in Taiwan 1626-1642: The Baroque Ending of a Renaissance Endeavour*. Hong Kong University Press, Hong Kong.

Calvin, J. B. (1984) *The China-India Border War*, Marine Corps Command and Staff College.

Chapuis, O. (1995) *A History of Vietnam from Hong Bang to Tu Duc*. Greenwood Publishing, Westport, Connecticut.

Chase, K. W. (2003) *Firearms: A Global History to 1700*. Cambridge University Press.

Cochrane, J. (2016) Indonesia protests Chinese aggression. In: *Internat'l New York Times,* Thursday, March 21.

Cooper, H. (2016). Jockeying for leverage in the South China Sea. in: *Internat'l New York Times,* Thursday, March 31. 2016, pp.1 & 5.

Data and Statistics (2015) World Economic Outlook Database; in *International Monetary Fund Publications,* October.

Dreyer, E. L. (2006) *Zheng He: China and the Oceans in the Early Ming Dynasty, 1404-1433*. Pearson Longman, London.

Easton, I. (2017) *The Chinese Invasion Threat: Taiwan's Defence and American Strategy in Asia.* The Project 2049 Institute, Arlington, Virginia.

Freeman, Jr., C. W. (Ambassador) (2010) *China's Challenge to American Hegemony.* Remarks to the global strategy forum at Middle East Policy Council. London.

Galambos, I. (2011) The Northern Neighbours of the Tangut; in *Cahiers de Linguistique – Asie Orientale.* Volume 40. CRLAO-EHESS, Paris.

Ghazarian, J. G. (2014) *Treasures of the Silk Road: The Religions that Transformed China.* New Generation Publishing, London.

Gibney, F. B. (2012) The Rise of State Capitalism; in *The Economist,* 21 January.

Gilpin, R. (1988) The Theory of Hegemonic War; in. *The Journal of Interdisciplinary History,* 18 (4).

Goldstein, J. S. (1997) *International Relations.* Pearson-Longman, New York.

Goldstein J. S. (2005) *International Relations.* Pearson-Longman, New York.

Gupta, K. (1971) The McMahon Line 1911–45: The British Legacy; in *The China Quarterly,* July-September.

Gyves, C. M. (1993) *An English Translation of General Oi Jiguang's "Ouanjing Jieyao Pian".* University of Arizona Press.

Hagstörm, L. (2008) Sino-Japanese Relations: The Ice That Won't Melt; in *International Journal.* Volume 64:1.

Hoare, J.E. (1995) *Japan's Treaty Ports and Foreign Settlements: The uninvited guests, 1858-1899.* Routledge, London.

Lamb, A. (1964) *The China-India Border.* Oxford University Press, London.

Lamb, A. (1966) *The McMahon line: a study in the relations between India, China and Tibet, 1904 to 1914.* Routledge, Toronto.

Leonard, M. (2008) *What Does China Think?* Harper Collins Publishers, London.

Mamdani, M. (2004) *Good Muslim, Bad Muslim: America, the Cold War, and the Roots of Terrorism.* Pantheon, New York.

Mao Tse Tung (1967) Report on an investigation on the peasant movement in Hunan, March1927; in *Selected Works of Mao Tse Tung.* Volume 1. Foreign Languages Press, Peking.

Mao Tse Tung (1967) Analysis of the classes in Chinese society, March 1926; in *Selected Works of Mao Tse Tung.* Volume 1. Foreign Languages Press, Peking.

Maxwell, N. (1970) *India's China War.* Jonathan Cape Ltd., London.

Maxwell, N. (1970) The Un-Negotiated Dispute; in *The China Quarterly,* No. 43.

McNeilly, M. R. (2001) *Sun Tzu and the Art of Modern Warfare.* Oxford University Press.

Needham, J. (1995) *Science and Civilization in China.* Volume 5, part 7. Cambridge University Press.

Nish, I. (1990) An Overview of Relations Between China and Japan, 1895-1945; in *China Quarterly,* Volume 124.

Riegl, M., Landovský, J., and Valko, I., (2014) *Strategic Regions in 21th Century Power Politics.* Cambridge Scholars Publishing.

Sawyer, R. D. (2007) *The Seven Military Classics of Ancient China.* Basic Books, New York.

Shakya, T. (1999). *The Dragon in the Land of Snows: A History of Modern Tibet Since 1947.* Columbia University Press, New York.

Sinha, P. B. and Athale, A. A. (1962) History of the Conflict with China; in (ed.) S.N. Prasad, *History Division,* Ministry of Defence Publ., Govt. of India, Delhi.

Van de Ven, Hans J. (2000) *Warfare in Chinese History. BRILL,* Leiden.

Wagstaff, A., Magnus, J., Xu, G. L. and Qian, J. (2009) Extending health insurance to the rural population: An impact evaluation of China's new cooperative medical scheme. *Journal of Health Economics.* No. 1.

Wang, Q. (2008) *Emperor Taizong of the Tang.* Chinese Social Sciences Press, Beijing.

Weidenbaum, M. L. (1996) *The Bamboo Network: How Expatriate Chinese Entrepreneurs are Creating a New Economic Superpower in Asia.* Martin Kessler Books, Free Press.

Woodman, D. (1969) *Himalayan Frontiers.* The Cresset Press, London.

Index

Index

Index

Index